INSIGHTS
ON PERSONAL GROWTH

VOLUME II

ADDITIONAL BOOKS BY THE AUTHOR

1. Adizes, I. *Industrial Democracy: Yugoslav Style*. New York Free Press, 1971.

2. Adizes, I. and E. Mann-Borgese, eds. *Self-Management: New Dimensions to Democracy*. Santa Barbara, CA: ABC-CLIO, 1975.

3. Adizes, I. *How to Solve the Mismanagement Crisis*. Homewood, IL: Dow Jones/ Irwin, 1979.

4. Adizes, I. *Corporate Lifecycles: How and Why Corporations Grow and Die and What to Do About It*. Englewood Cliffs, NJ: Prentice Hall, 1988.

5. Adizes, I. *Mastering Change: The Power of Mutual Trust and Respect in Personal Life,Family Life, Business & Society*. Santa Monica, CA: Adizes Institute, 1991.

6. Adizes, I. *Managing Corporate Lifecycles*: *An updated and expanded look at the Corporate Lifecycles.* First printing, Paramus, NJ: Prentice Hall Press, 1999. Additional printings by the Adizes Institute Publications.

7. Adizes, I. *Pursuit of Prime*. First printing Santa Monica, CA: Knowledge Exchange, 1996. Additional printings by the Adizes Institute Publications.

8. Adizes, I. *The Ideal Executive: Why You Cannot Be One and What to Do About It*. Santa Barbara, CA: The Adizes Institute Publications, 2004.

9. Adizes, I. *Management/Mismanagement Styles: How to Identify a Style and What to Do About It*. Santa Barbara, CA: The Adizes Institute Publications, 2004.

10. Adizes, I. *Leading the Leaders: How to Enrich Your Style of Management and Handle People Whose Style is Different from Yours*. Santa Barbara, CA: The Adizes Institute Publications, 2004.

11. Adizes, I. *How to Manage in Times of Crisis (And How to Avoid a Crisis in the First Place)*. Santa Barbara, CA: The Adizes Institute Publications, 2009.

12. Adizes, I. *Insights on Management*. Santa Barbara, CA: The Adizes Institute Publications, 2011.

13. Adizes, I. *Insights on Policy*. Santa Barbara, CA: The Adizes Institute Publications, 2011.

14. Adizes, I. *Insights on Personal Growth*. Santa Barbara, CA: The Adizes Institute Publications, 2011.

15. Adizes, I. *Food for Thought: On Management*. Santa Barbara, CA: The Adizes Institute Publications, 2013.

16. Adizes, I. *Food for Thought: On Change and Leadership*. Santa Barbara, CA: The Adizes Institute Publications, 2013.

17. Adizes, I. *Food for Thought: On What Counts in Life*. Santa Barbara, CA: The Adizes Institute Publications, 2013.

INSIGHTS

ON PERSONAL GROWTH

GROWTH

VOLUME II

ICHAK KALDERON ADIZES

Founder and CEO, Adizes Institute

Santa Barbara County, California

Library of Congress Cataloging-in-Publication Data

Adizes, Ichak.
Insights on Personal Growth, Volume 11

Library of Congress Control Number Pending

ISBN: 978-0-937-120-28-6

Published by Adizes Institute Publications
1212 Mark Avenue
Carpinteria, Santa Barbara County, California, USA 93013
805-565-2901; Fax 805-565-0741
Website: www.adizes.com

Design and layout by Dana Levy, Perpetua Press
Printed in the United States of America

Additional copies may be ordered from www.adizes.com/store

dedicated to
Dr. Allan Goldhamer
who has been saving my life with
his invaluable advice

CONTENTS

INTRODUCTION   11

PART I: HEALTHY LIVING

Acting Outside of the Box   15

Are Cigarette Warnings Good for You?   18

Feel to Feel   20

How to Avoid Jet Lag   23

How to Resist Temptation   25

On Being Obese   27

On Change, Obesity and Weight Loss   29

PAEI and Hygienic Living   31

Taking Care of Oneself   34

Tody que Es Demasyadu No Valle   37

What Is a Vacation?   39

Who Should Rest?   41

PART II: RELATIONSHIPS

What Is the Biggest Asset in a Marriage?   47

Expressions of Love   50

What Women and Men Want   52

Maintaining a Marriage   54

The Institution of Marriage   56

Lifecycle of a Marriage   59

Marriage as a School   61

What Makes a Person Attractive?   64

The Discomfort of Being Rich   66

Why Being Creative Is Dangerous   68

On Father's Day   70

Father-Son Conflicts   73

Part III: Self-Knowledge

Awareness, Consciousness and Conscience   79

More on Awareness, Consciousness and Conscience   82

Dealing with Anger   85

Denying Death   88

Duality and Oneness   90

More About Duality   92

Caging the Ego   95

Love and Life   98

The Relation of Love and Change   100

One More Time on Love   102

What Is Love All About, Anyway?   104

What Causes Trust, and Its Implications   106

What Is Truth?   109

When No Is a Yes   111

The Impact of the Holocaust   113

The Wonderful Life of Not Expecting   115

On Loving Yourself and Others   118

Part IV: Spirituality

About Life and Death   123

Is There Life After Death?   125

How I Found God   126

On Jesus Christ   136

Reflections on Christmas   139

On Forgiving Wishes for the New Year   140

Insights from Passover Night   143

What Makes Us Human?   147

Reflections from My Stay in an Ashram   149

When Do We Die?   152

Part V: Tools for Life

All Problems Are Just a Test   157

Life Is a Game of Cards   159

Life Is Conflicts, Flirtations and Pain. Necessarily So?   161

My Jazz Revelation   163

On Diversity   167

The European Soccer Cup Games   169

The Meaning of Money   170

The Wall: An Allegory   173

There Are No Mistakes   176

To Love What I Hate   178

Too Lazy to Think   180

Look for What You Do Not See   182

Who Gets the Most Gives the Least   184

Why Not to Expect Nor to Want   186

About the Adizes Institute   191

Introduction

I AM AWARE that there is a certain amount of hubris in my publishing a book of insights on personal growth. After all, I am a management consultant with a Ph.D. in Business Administration and a large amount of experience dealing with organizational psychology. But personal affairs and spiritual concerns? Family matters and the relationship between fathers and sons, husbands and wives—isn't that a bit of stretch?

Actually I think not. First, my theories of change, lifecycles and relationships within the managerial field have broader application than solely to the business world. They yield an approach and a systematic method that applies as well to relationships, personal as well as corporate. Second, much of my focus and experience deals with process and behavior, and seems applicable in a large range of fields. I also draw few boundaries between my professional and my personal life. They meet at the edge and merge for me, one reinforcing the other. I tell many of my clients and their corporate managers that unless their private lives are in balance and harmony it will be difficult for them to manage the changes and pressures required to perform successfully within the business world.

I should add to this that I am a man of infinite curiosity. I have consulted with psychiatrists of many persuasions and approaches over a period of twenty years, searching with them for greater understanding of what occurs in the exchanges between human beings, particularly the intense ones that are associated with families and domestic life. I have also sought inspiration and refuge from spiritual advisers; indeed am a follower of Master Chariji, the spiritual leader of Sahag Marg meditation; I have met with him a number of times in his spiritual home in the Himalayas in Northern India.

My curiosity has also taken me to different parts of the world—more populated than the Himalayas, I might add—where I have met with political leaders and simple working men and women. Invariably I have found that their personal and family issues were often reflections of the complex organizational problems I was looking into within their native land.

And so, from one week to the next, as I traveled the world (I am away from my home in Southern California about eighty percent of the time), I have set down my personal observations. Hence this book, which is the second volume of personal insights and covers my experiences and thoughts derived from them since 2012. I am particularly proud that many of these insights were derived from contact with men and women in the developing countries of the world, where the impact of globalization is felt so intensely…and with, it seems to me, so much wisdom.

Readers of my blog who may have encountered some of these pieces in their original form may find there are occasional changes. Part of this is a function of changes in my experience, and the thinking that has accompanied these changes. And part, of course, is a reflection of input from my readers.

A word here about the Adizes Institute, where I am the Director and CEO, and on whose website these blogs first appeared. Unlike much of the work of the Institute these blogs were not the product of research and theory, but rather were just what I called them, insights; aperçus or perceptions that emanated from the rather extraordinary access to the world that my professional life has afforded me.

Whether you are a new or a seasoned and familiar reader, I invite you, as always, to respond to these perceptions and insights of mine.

The end in mind is a dialogue, not a soliloquy.

Ichak Kalderon Adizes, Ph.D.

PART I

❃

HEALTHY LIVING

ACTING OUTSIDE OF THE BOX[1]

IN HIS SEMINAL BOOK *LATERAL THINKING* [2], Dr. Edward De Bono coined the phrase "to think outside of the box."

I would like to discuss some examples in which I solved a problem by not just thinking out of the box but by acting out of the box, in the hope that you, my readers, might find them helpful.

Homeopathy

This occurred about twenty years ago: I had a terrific pain in my right heel. I could not stand, which I need to do—sometimes for eight straight hours—when I lecture or consult. It was a serious problem.

The first doctor I went to was a specialist in sports medicine who diagnosed the culprit as a tight ligament and treated me with cortisone injections.

The pain stopped for a few days; then it came back.

The next doctor was a foot specialist. He concluded that I was walking incorrectly and needed to visit his office twice a week in order to relearn how to walk. I, in turn, concluded that he probably had a child whose college tuition he needed to finance, so I went to a third doctor.

By then, almost a year had passed, during which I was in continual pain.

The third doctor took an X-ray of my heel and concluded that I had a spur—an abnormal bone growth—and needed to have surgery to remove it.

1. Adizes Insights, April 2011.

2. Dr. Edward De Bono, *Lateral Thinking*. New York: Harper & Row, 1970.

Luckily, before the surgery, I met a homeopathic doctor at a yoga center and told him about my heel pain.

Almost a year had passed, during which I was in continual pain.

He did not take X-rays. He did not even examine my heel. He asked me some apparently unrelated questions about my working and leisure habits. Then he told me to hold my heel in my hand, close my eyes, and imagine my heel as a son whom I love more than myself, and to send love to my heel. It was strange, but I did as instructed.

Then he gave me two small pills and told me to put them under my tongue and allow them to dissolve. I did.

That afternoon my pain disappeared and has never come back.

Tibetan massage

About a year and a half ago, I was lifting weights as exercise. Either I was too eager or I did it the wrong way, because I pulled something in my right shoulder.

That was serious for me, because when I lecture or consult I often write on overhead projectors and flip charts. Now I could not lift my hand without causing excruciating pain in my shoulder.

I went to an orthopedic surgeon, who took X-rays and, as expected, recommended surgery.

I decided against it, and went to a chiropractor for weekly massages instead. The pain lessened but did not disappear. But at least I could use my arm.

A physical therapist recommended certain exercises. My shoulder improved, but the pain could still be felt constantly.

Two months ago in Moscow, a Tibetan masseur gave me a massage. When I told him about my pain, he massaged my shoulder, then treated me with "sucking cups."

First he sucked the air out of the cups using burning cotton on a metal stick, then placed the cups against my shoulder. They seemed to actually suck my muscle back into its proper position.

That is it. The pain was gone and has not come back—at least not yet—and my shoulder is fully operational.

Third experience

Last month, I heard a whistle in my right ear. It started as a quiet hum, but after a few days it became a shrill whistle that drove me absolutely crazy. There was no way to stop it, no place to escape it. My concentration was ruined. How could I lecture? How could I write or read or even have a conversation?

I went to an ear specialist. After doing an MRI and confirming that I did not have a tumor in my brain, he told me there was no cure for this problem and suggested that I try distracting myself by listening to music.

Under medical supervision, she was put on a water fast for forty-one days.

I was desperate. Fortunately, I met Zdenko Domancic, in Slovenia, who does bio-energetic healing. I told him about the noise in my ear. One of his students treated me without even touching my ear. Just manipulating the energy around my ear. The whistle stopped. It has been now more than two years since then and the whistle has not returned.

Christina

The three stories above are my personal experiences. If you want more "outside of the box" stories, go to www.truenorthhealth.com and watch the video about Christina, whose brain was damaged when a falling beam hit her on the head. For eighteen years she had terrible, continuous headaches. The various doctors who examined her all agreed on the diagnosis and told her no medicine or treatment was possible.

After eighteen years of excruciating pain, she came to True North Health Center, in Santa Rosa, California. Under medical supervision, she was put on a water fast for forty-one days. Not only did she lose fifty pounds of extra weight, she lost the headache too. Needless to say, she looks terrific.

Some people come to True North with what seems like incurable lupus and leave symptom-free.

Are Cigarette Warnings Good for You?[1]

I AM NOT A SMOKER. I mean, I do not smoke *my* cigarettes. If someone is smoking next to me, I grab one or two and take a drag.

I have noticed, though, that there is pattern to when I do pick up a cigarette. Yes, it goes with a cup of coffee, but mostly it is when I am tense, stressed, or tired.

> *They subconsciously encourage me to smoke.*

And I ignore the sign that says that cigarettes kill. As a matter of fact, I think the warnings have the *opposite* effect: They subconsciously encourage me to smoke.

They *enable* the practice.

Strange, no?

How?

Why?

When I am tired and stressed I have this deep need to stop the pain, to die. So I overeat although I know it is not good for my health. And I smoke.

Aha. Maybe the warning reinforces this desire to die and confirms that I am doing the "right" thing.

If I am correct about this insight, then the more stressed a society is the more smoking there will be. And if smoking is prohibited or too expensive, alcohol or marijuana becomes the substitute. Or other drugs that make you forget who you are or what is happening to you. And if you are continuously stressed and need this form of relief, it is no longer a relief.

1. Adizes Insights, December 2013.

It becomes an addiction, and our hidden, temporary need to destroy ourselves becomes an ongoing process of killing ourselves prematurely.

So what is the effective intervention that will stop us smoking and destroying our health?

It is not the warning signs. Go for the cause, not the effect. Stop the stress. Meditate. Do yoga. And don't take life too seriously. Hang loose, as they say in Hawaii, and may you live a long life and stop all attempts to have it shortened.

FEEL TO FEEL[1]

I WAS WATCHING A MOTHER soothing her crying child when I realized that very few words passed between the two. Hardly any at all. The mother was holding her daughter close to her chest, kissing and caressing her lightly. The only sounds I could hear were soft murmurs of love.

I thought to myself, at the end of the day, we are all children at heart.

When we are in pain, all we want is to be loved, caressed, held close to the heart, comforted by someone we love. Not words. At those moments of hurt and anguish words only interfere with our need to feel and be felt.

It has long been a truism in our culture that women do not want someone reasoning with them when they are feeling despondent or simply feeling low. Logical investigation of why they hurt and what to do about it often only leads to anger, if not fury.

What is wanted is that we shut up and listen.

What is wanted is that we shut up and listen. What is wanted is emotional touching, not reason; love, not logic; a sense that the person they care about connects to their feelings, not their mind. What I call "feel to feel."

But, come to think of it, we men need and desire the same kind of response.

Imagine for a moment a man coming home from some interaction in the office that went badly. Our partner tries to talk us out of how we feel; tries to use logic; tries to persuade us not to be so bruised or unhappy or out of sorts.

I believe our response is predictable: We would be furious.

1. Adizes Insights, August 2013.

Just shut up and feel my pain is what we want too, although often we are unable to utter the words, too macho to ask for comfort. But wouldn't it be nice if our partner just held us, hugged us, listened to us, and was "just there?"

If an insight is called for here, it might be stated as:

> Logical issues should be handled with logic, and feelings should be handled with feelings. Not feelings with logic or logic with feelings.

Here are some examples of potential confusion:

Think of a person dying. Imagine someone telling him that it is not so terrible. Really. There is life after death. God is waiting. And, come to think of it, heaven is not a bad place to be. It is so idiotic that it is not even funny…an extreme example of feelings handled with logic, with words.

Something else is wanted here. Something simple. And direct. Perhaps as slight a gesture as holding someone's hand. Silently. With a caress. Or placing a hand on his or her heart. Gazing directly at one another.

It becomes a way of showing love. Of transmitting your sense of caring. Do not speak. Talk will only interfere, will only blur the connection.

Feelings should be responded to with feelings.

By the same token we should handle logical issues not with feelings but with logic.

Imagine that you come to someone and ask him for advice, explaining what went wrong. Instead of reasoning with you, offering alternate suggestions or possible paths to follow, he tries to hold your hand, hugs you in an effort to offer comfort, and tries to make you feel better. You would dismiss that person in a heartbeat. You were seeking advice, not emotional support; tough analytical reasoning, not sympathy or empathy.

The rule is: Feelings should be responded with feelings and logic with logic. Do not confuse which stimulus calls for which response.

Look at lovers sitting on a bench by the beach at sunset. Is he saying, "Let me tell you the many ways *why* I love you," or is he just holding her in an embrace and not saying a word?

Speaking would ruin the moment.

Feelings come from the heart and, yes, there is and can be heart-to-heart communion. Without declaring a sentence or uttering a word.

The mind speaks with words; the heart with action done in silence.

To me this insight, which evolved as I watched a mother soothe a crying child, has repercussions within a marriage, in a lover's fight, and even in a business partnership turning sour.

Because what hurts people, more times than we understand, is not what happens to them but what it means to them. Often it is the heart that is reacting to what is going on, not necessarily the mind.

Less talk, more heartfelt action. To help someone in that situation we need first to empathize. When he calms down and asks for our comments, in effect wants us to speak, only then should we respond with words of understanding. But not sooner.

If this insight makes sense, it has repercussions in international relations as well. For example, today there is still no peace in the Middle East. I suggest that there will be none until both sides are able and willing to respond to each other with "heart speak" not "mind speak," with actions from the heart and not words expressing the mind.

What is happening instead is that words of negotiation have become the form and substance of exchange. They have covered over and replaced the feeling side of the equation. What they have left on the table is all barter and logic; rational thinking; who did what to whom; who is the victim and who is the villain.

All the while the real problem is staring us (and them) in the face: Jewish hearts bleeding from the Holocaust, and Palestinian hearts torn by the loss of home and land.

I am not suggesting here that they hold hands and look into one another's eyes. Please…but there are ways I believe each side can turn to one another with an open heart. Less talk, more heartfelt action.

Here is an example: A friend of mine who is the personal physician of Shimon Peres, the President of Israel, does exactly that. Once a month he and dozens of physicians visit a different Palestinian village and offer their medical services free of charge. That seems to me a feel-to-feel act. A response from the heart; less talk and more heartfelt action

If there is going to be peace in a marriage, in a partnership going sour, in international relations, the path must lead from the heart…and include far fewer words. At least to start with.

How to Avoid Jet Lag[1]

MY MOST RECENT TRIP started in Santa Rosa, California, where I spent one month at the True North Health Center, learning to keep to a strict SOS Vegan diet: no Salt, no Oil, no Sugar, and no animal products (meat, fish, fowl, eggs, or dairy). Just vegetables and fruit, and, for starch, potatoes, rice, and other grains.

I went there to get rid of my high blood pressure.

From Santa Rosa, I went to Moscow via San Francisco and Houston.

I was in Russia for one week, spending long days leading more than thirty Russian managers through a problem-solving session, communicating in Russian by using a simultaneous translator. Stressful.

Afterward, I flew to Mexico, to the Adizes Conference in Guadalajara. You would expect that my jet lag would be severe, right? But this time, for the first time in my life (and I have been flying regularly for forty years), I had *no* jet lag. I arrived in Mexico and went to work right away.

I also slept very well for eight hours each night. Usually with jet lag, I sleep badly, waking up every two to three hours, and I am disoriented for several days.

I wondered what had made the difference.

After a week working every day at the convention in Guadalajara, I flew on to Monterrey, Mexico, to work with a multinational billion-dollar company. I had thirty Mexican executives whose problems I was help-ing to solve, for which I had to make the transition to communicating in Spanish.

1. Adizes Insights, February 2011.

More work. More stress. Still not tired. Still full of energy. What was going on?

When I finished up in Monterrey, I flew to New Delhi, India. This was a long trip. First I flew to Houston, waited a few hours there, then took another flight to Newark, New Jersey. After waiting some more, I boarded the thirteen-hour flight to India.

Then I realized: It is the diet!
I should have been half dead by then, right? Not at all. I was still full of energy. I was ready to work immediately upon landing, and slept a full eight hours.

What the heck is going on, I wondered. Then I realized: It is the diet! It's eating vegetables, lots of green vegetables.

Wow! If you ask the man on the street what gives you more energy, meat or vegetables, the answer would be "meat." People expect meat to create more energy because it has more concentrated calories than vegetables. But if you think like a businessman, you'll realize that what counts is not just revenues but profits, which means you must take costs into account.

In dieting use the same principle: Meat gives you lots of energy, granted, but consider how much energy it consumes being processed and digested. What is left for you to use? Very, very little. That is why, after a heavy meat-based meal, you feel sleepy.

Vegetables, on the other hand, have fewer calories, but also consume very few calories in the digestion process, leaving lots of energy that you can use.

Whoa! What a discovery! I fly more than 200 days a year across multiple time zones, rarely staying in one time zone for more than few days. I have been chronically tired for as long as I can remember. And now, at age 73, I have found the spring of youth, the source of energy. Hello, everyone! It is vegetables! With no dressing, no oil, no salt, no sugar, and no animal products.

Is the diet easy to sustain? The first twenty-one days are very difficult. But after those three weeks, when your taste buds have adjusted, the food tastes delicious; there is nothing more tasty than the true taste of nature.

How to Resist Temptation[1]

PROFESSOR DEBORAH MACINNIS, a professor and Vice Dean for Research and Strategy at the University of Southern California Marshall School of Business in Los Angeles, has done some fascinating research that may have significant applications for management.

She and a colleague tested responses to temptation under different circumstances: She placed three groups of people in a room containing a delicious-looking chocolate cake and the implements to divide and eat it.

The first group was put into the room and told to think about the shame and guilt they would feel if they ate the cake.

The second was told to think about how proud they would be of *not* eating it.

The third group, the control group, was put in the room and given no instructions.

Here were the results:

The control group ate the most. The group that was told to think about pride ate the least.

MacInnis concluded that shame and guilt do not work as well as a sense of pride to help resist temptation.

I believe I know why: Shame and guilt *consume* energy, subtracting energy from our will to resist temptation. Pride, on the other hand, *gives* energy, allocating more energy to the willpower to resist.

Interesting, isn't it?

1. Adizes Insights, July 2011.

This has definite implications for resisting common faults such as over-eating, procrastinating, and being lazy.

In life, we are often confronted with the temptation to do something pleasurable that we know is unhealthy or unwise.

How can we overcome those temptations? By comparing the pleasure of doing it with the pleasure and pride we get from *not* doing it.

On Being Obese[1]

THE MEDICAL DEFINITION OF OBESITY is that your height-to-weight ratio or body fat is a certain number. You need to lose weight or else....

The "else" is quite ominous: disease, early death, difficulty sitting in a small chair, paying for two seats on an airplane, and, possibly, having quite a miserable sex life.

You wonder which is worse....

So we need to lose weight.

How?

Go on a diet.

Good.

How?

After trying a dozen diets, I found one that works: SOS Vegan. No meat, fish, fowl, dairy, eggs, salt, sugar, or any fats.

In a month I lost fifteen pounds.

How do you sustain it? Aha. That is where the problem is. It is not in losing weight but in keeping it off.

I found what causes me to get off the diet:

When I am sleep deprived (especially because of jet lag).
When I am stressed.
When I am tired.

What happens then?

1. Adizes Insights, November 2012.

I feel miserable. I need something to pick me up. I look for some pleasure in my life. And I turn to food. Rich food. Salty or sweet food. With olive oil. And concentrated calories.

What is the insight?

I look for some pleasure in my life. That people who are fat and obese are miserable. Not happy-go-lucky. The myth is that overweight people are happy and skinny people are miserable. Maybe it was true a hundred years ago when people were not conscious that fat is no good for you. My grandfather and grandmother were obese but that was considered, in the society of the time, a sign of success. That they had made it in life. Skinny people were the losers. Those who did not have enough to eat.

The world changed.

Who overeats? Those who feel miserable, stressed, tired, sleepless. Those who look for some pleasure in life, which they do not have otherwise.

On Change, Obesity, and Weight Loss[1]

THERE IS AN EPIDEMIC OF OBESITY in the United States. In spite of a multimillion-dollar industry dedicated to weight loss, statistics show that weight-loss plans have a pretty bad success rate.

What is going on?

Here is my insight:

There is change. (Surprise, surprise!)

Change causes stress.

Stress makes us look for something that will compensate us with pleasure.

Pleasures are alcohol, smoking, and eating.

I will focus here on eating.

The food industry works very hard to make food pleasurable and cheap, and thus affordable.

How do they make it pleasurable? By adding salt everywhere possible, for instance, although it is *not healthy*.

How do they make it cheap? Process the food with the cheapest ingredients, which means it is not nourishing but it has lots of calories.

What happens now?

When you consume high calorie, pleasurable, non-nourishing food, you want more of it and since it is cheap you consume lots of it.

The result: obesity.

Notice the sequence of my reasoning:

Change >> stress >> pleasure seeking >> non-nourishing, cheap, tasty food >> more and more of it >> obesity.

1. Adizes Insights, February 2013.

So my argument is that obesity is caused by the high rate of change. Change is the root cause.

Go to a small village where life moves slowly. You will not see many obese people. They eat. They do not starve. And they are not on diets. They are not so stressed.

Maybe you can stop seeking pleasure.

Now go to a developed country where the rate of change is off the charts and walk the streets. Lots of obese people.

What to do?

You cannot stop change. It is tough to reduce stress, too. You can try. Good luck.

Aha. Maybe you can stop seeking pleasure.

How?

Not by moving to a cave and meditating all day long. Not by denouncing the world of pleasure. It is part of the American constitution that we have the right to be happy. So this will not work.

What to do?

Replace bad pleasures with healthy good pleasures.

My friend Bob Nemer produces and sells a powder made of dried, ground vegetables and fruits that, mixed with water and ice, tastes great. It immediately reduces hunger.

If you eat lots of vegetables to start with, and fill your stomach with them, your hunger for anything else declines. But there is a catch: Because they are low in calories you will be hungry sooner than later. So carry some baked potatoes with you.

PAEI and Hygienic Living[1]

L IVING HYGIENICALLY means nurturing conditions that promote health, either to prevent disease or to cure the root of the disease.

Typical Western medicine is not necessarily hygienic.

Taking aspirin for a headache, for instance, does not cure the causes of the headache; you are not having a headache because you are aspirin deficient. This solution removes the headache but not the problem that caused the headache in the first place. If any "curing" is going on in such a situation it is the body curing itself.

Thus, the conditions that enable the body to treat itself have to be created—that is called hygienic living.

The basic principles of hygienic living are sleep, exercise, and diet.

I have been thinking that we are back to PAEI again. Exercise will be (P), diet (A), and sleep (I).

How did I come to this classification?

Exercise deals with the body's functions. Thus it is most like a (P) function, a "doer." For diet, you have to control what you eat, and control is (A). During sleep the body integrates, relaxes, and rejuvenates, which is an (I) process.

I realize this classification is very subjective, and might even look arbitrary, but it serves my argument that what is missing in hygienic living, I think, is purpose, the (E).

To live hygienically one has to also have a *purpose* in life. Viktor Frankl has made this point well in his book[2]. He found that the people who

---

1. Adizes Insights, December 2011.

2. *Man's Search for Meaning*, Boston: Beacon Press, 1959.

survived the extermination camps in which he was a prisoner were people who had meaning in their lives, who had a reason to live.

We also know from the many annals of medical studies—and personal
experience as well—that people who have a purpose to fulfill, a future
life on earth that they still envision, survive diseases better than those
who give up and feel that there is no more use for them and no reason
to live.

For hygienic living, a way of living that prolongs life and decreases the
chances of self-inflicted diseases and maladies—I am not referring here
to car accidents or breaking bones—the body must be allowed to self-
heal and re-integrate itself. We, as humans, need deep sleep that follows
the body's natural rhythms, which means no alarm clocks. The body
needs to go to sleep when it is tired and wake up when it is ready. The
sleep also has to be without interferences—no noise, light, or TV programs—and with good ventilation and a moderate, cool temperature.

Hygienic sleep, exercise, and proper diet are not enough.

For exercise, there are three main areas of
importance: aerobic conditioning, which
works the heart muscle and allows blood
to flow to the whole body; strength training, which works the heart in yet another
manner, and increases the body's ability to
perform aerobic exercise; and, last but not least, flexibility and balance,
which are especially important the more one ages to maintain peak mo-
bility and comfort.

As for diet, there are as many recommended as there are medical experts.
I am convinced that the vegan diet, with the added conditions of no sugar,
salt, or fat, provides the greatest health benefits.

As I said above, however, hygienic sleep, exercise, and proper diet are
not enough. One needs to have a mission in life, a purpose. Without it
we age rapidly, we lose energy, and we lose the desire to live. It is this
spirit, drive, or (E), that gives (P), (A), and (I) a purpose to be.

Look what happens to people who retire but have not planned what to do
with their lives in the aftermath. Watch how fast their health deteriorates.

What is the purpose in life when one retires? What is the mission? How
does one define it?

As one ages it looks more and more difficult to define a mission because making money and sustaining a career are no longer the purpose. Raising a family? The kids are gone and independent now.

So what to do?

I've found in my consulting profession an answer which makes sense for corporations, but it is *also* applicable to personal life:

Only cancer serves no one but itself. Do not ask yourself *why* you live, and *why* you are on this planet, and *what* is life all about. These questions have no real answer because they have no real focus; they are too open-ended.

The word *why* in the four languages I speak is synonym for *what for*, like in Spanish: *porque*, *paraque*. In Slavic languages: *za sto*, *zasto*. In Hebrew: *lama*, *l'ma*.

So, replace the *why* and ask yourself *what for* are you in this world?

And what is that *what for*?

Notice that every organ in our body exists to serve another part of the body. Only cancer serves no one but itself. Thus cancer serves death. To live, the parts have to serve the total, or at least other parts of the system.

It makes sense then to substitute *what for* with the question *for whom*.

When you were building a career you knew for whom you lived: for the clients your career was serving so that your practice would grow. When you were building a family you were living for each other and the children.

As you age, the career is over. The nest is empty. What now? Do you live for the grandchildren? I suggest you see them, enjoy them, but if you live for them your kids will resent your interference.

So for whom?

To prolong your life, to live a healthy life, to have a purpose to live, find a cause you believe in with all your heart. Dedicate your life to it. Volunteer your time. Do not just sign a check and send it; that will not do it. Give of your time. Have a reason to get up in the morning.

When I consult to companies I ask them: "Who will cry if you die, if the company goes bankrupt?" That is for whom you live. The same applies in personal life. When you retire, to prolong life, live hygienically—and find someone or something you care for, someone or something that truly needs you to be alive, and you will live longer.

Taking Care of Oneself[1]

I AM A SURVIVOR OF THE HOLOCAUST. I was six years old when we were taken to a concentration camp. After the war, I actually went hungry until the age of eleven when we immigrated to Israel. But there I did not have it easy either. I had to work from the age of eleven to support my family.

All in all, I had no childhood.

This has become clear to me only as I am writing my autobiography.

I came to the realization that by having no carefree childhood, I do not know what it is to just have fun and do nothing. I never did. I do not know what it is to just be happy. I never experienced that.

I was talking to a neurolinguistic coach. I told her about this revelation I arrived at as I was writing my book.

She asked me if I have a picture of myself from that age, from the time of the war.

I said I do. And, come to think of it, I look so sad in that picture. In it I am a little kid being hugged by an older girl whom I loved. She was a daughter of an Italian officer and only two or three years older than me. (At the time it was taken, Italy occupied Pristina, the place we were hiding.) I was so scared she would discover that I was Jewish and her father would kill us all. I could not smile, not even for a picture.

The coach suggested I take this picture with me wherever I go, and commit myself to taking care of this little kid who never had a childhood. My name growing up was Izzy. "So to take care of Izzy," she told me, "imagine you are his father now. What would you do for him?" she asked.

1. Adizes Insights, August 2012.

That afternoon I took Izzy for a walk around the lake. We were in Bled, Slovenia. I held his hand, and we talked. Talked for a long time. I bought him an ice cream. I told him not to be scared anymore, that I will be there for him for as long as I live. And that I would never let him down. I told him that I love him very much and hope that he will eventually smile, because life does offer opportunities to smile and love.

I had the best time ever.

I hugged little Izzy and promised to take him on another walk soon.

What happened here?

"Me" and "I" are not the same. "I" have to take care of "Me."

How "close" are you to your childhood?

Let me explain.

Adizes Theory says success is from the inside out. This formula has a meaning in personal life, too. Not just business.

How "close" are you to your childhood? Close your eyes and imagine yourself as a kid. How does it feel?

Let us go beyond memories.

Are you in touch with your heart?

I remember a doctor once gave me his stethoscope to listen to my own heart. He asked me: "Can you hear your heartbeat? It is beating for *you*."

I cried. Yes I did. I am not ashamed to admit it. That heart was there working so hard to keep me alive, and I never paid attention to it.

I have been taking my heart for granted. And my kidneys for granted. And my lungs for granted. I have never stopped to ask them: "Hey, how do you feel?" Never took real care of them. They were there with me from the day I was born—like little Izzy has been with me for a long time—but I never paid attention to them. They were "there" some-where, like passengers on a bus I drove. They were not "Me." They were "them."

All my life "Me" was my brain. That is it. Just a brain. A walking brain. All the others were passengers. I identified only with my brain and wor-ried only about him. Sad, but true.

It is an interesting idea, but what now?

Take care of the little Izzy in you. When you get up ask your heart, "Hello, how are you today?" And your lungs, and your body. And your emotions, too: "How do we feel today?"

Start the day "together," otherwise in the rush of modern life, your body goes one way, your mind another way, and your emotions go to hell.

Periodically bring your "Me" family—mind, body, and emotions—together. Let your spirit do the integration.

Do that consciously. As a ritual.

Now, when I finish taking a shower I stop and check my body. Check my skin. I put some lotion on my body, and check it if it is okay. And shave slowly. And check my face. And smile at myself. And feel okay about getting older.

It is a full-time job to love oneself.

Tody que Es Demasyadu No Valle[1]

THE ABOVE TITLE IS A SEPHARDIC SPANISH expression from the Middle Ages, which means: "All that is exaggerated is no good."

Once I had dinner with a prominent medical doctor. Since I am interested in organizational health, I asked him to define health in one word, if he could.

He said: "Moderation."

"Berries are healthy, right? But if you eat only berries you will get sick," he said.

Now think about it.

To be healthy, we need sleep, exercise, and a proper diet.

Now let us exaggerate and over-exercise. Push it further, and then still further, and you can see how a person might become sick.

Same with sleep. Overdo it and you turn into an Oblomov, a fictitious character from nineteenth-century Russian literature who spent most of his life in bed.

How about exaggerating with the proper diet?

Let us start with vegetarians. Now move to the next extreme and you have vegans, men and women who refrain from eating any animal products. Push it to another level of exaggeration and you are suddenly in the land of the SOS Vegan, a vegan who also cuts sugar, oil, and salt from his diet. What is next? The raw food enthusiasts who are like SOS Vegans, but will not cook anything. Next we are down to the raw food enthusiasts who refuse to eat tomatoes and eggplant—they consider them to be

1. Adizes insights, May 2013.

toxic. If you progress any further, you will wind up eating only berries, and the next thing you know, you are anorexic.

In short, pursue health to the extreme and you will become sick.

The wisdom of the Sephardic Middle Ages has repercussions in politics, as well. Take the concept of democracy. Free speech. Free political affiliation. Freedom of assembly. Carried to an extreme an un-democratic party can gain power in democratic ways and destroy democracy. That is what Hitler did.

I believe that is what is happening in Europe today, specifically in the Scandinavian countries, and particularly in Sweden.

It is now illegal to have a single Swedish culture.

In the name of being anti-racist, the Swedish government has changed the constitution so that it is now illegal to have a single Swedish culture. Multiculturalism is now required; it's the order of the day.

Sounds good. Very liberal. Humanistic.

But can it mean that fanatic Islamists can flourish, protected by the constitution, and slowly but surely change the country until there is only a single Islamic culture?

Why this phenomenon of moving to extremes?

I believe it is because people want a formula, do not want uncertainty, do not want to think and handle the uncertainty that comes with making a decision. As if saying, "Just tell me what to do, give me instructions so I do not have to think." (A) behavior. They do not use common sense. When people have a formula to follow they do not have to think any more. And as they follow the formula blindly, it becomes more and more extreme by default.

The greater the rate of change, the greater the uncertainty, the more people need rules to guide them; to tell them how to behave. Simple rules. Simple directions which provide security and certainty. But when pushed to an extreme, simple rules often lead to results that are opposite the ones intended.

What Is a Vacation?[1]

M Y WIFE AND I TOOK A VACATION this week. We went to visit a friend of mine and his wife who have a chalet in Chamonix, France. From my window I could see Mont Blanc.

It occurred to me that the last—and only—vacation I have had was more than fifty years ago, in 1957, when I graduated from high school and was sent to a youth camp in France.

Before that, from the age of eleven, I worked every summer to help the family financially. Until I was eleven, World War II was in progress.

After 1957, as a university and graduate student, I worked every summer. Once I became a professor, and later a consultant, I did take "vacations," but I realize now that they were not vacations.

Why?

A vacation means not *working*. For me, since my work involves constant thinking, it is my brain that needs a break. A true vacation is not *thinking*. Until now, none of my vacations has rested my brain.

Why? Because I love my work so much that it is like an addiction. I am constantly looking for "pips"—potential improvement points—in any situation, looking for what is wrong and what can and should be improved.

For instance, I once went to Club Med for a vacation. But within two days, I had started consulting to the chief of the village and ended up working right through the vacation. For free.

And I had *paid* for this "vacation."

1. Adizes Insights, July 2011.

Even when I was not consulting—when I went to Paris for a week, for example, we went to the theater, to museums, restaurants—my mind never got a break. I was constantly analyzing how everything was organized and what could be improved.

Here in Chamonix, we went hiking. We experienced nature. Here, finally, is where my mind was given a rest.

Why?

In nature everything is as should be. It is perfect as it is. Human intervention cannot improve it. There are no improvement points.

In nature you experience beauty—which is a *feeling*, not a *thought*. Your heart takes over, and your brain gets a break.

Natural beauty cannot be explained; it can only be experienced.

Like God. God cannot be explained, either; only experienced.

It is not strange that poets and philosophers urge us to experience nature. In nature, you feel present. You stop thinking about the past or future. Nature overwhelms you, and you find yourself totally present, experiencing the *now*.

Letting your heart take over, letting it speak, feel, and be, is a real vacation—a vacation for your *brain*.

Are there alternatives to nature?

Sure. Any experience that makes you *feel* and not think. Any experience that makes you forget about the past or the future and brings you to the *now*. Like dancing. Painting. Singing. That is a vacation.

Think which parts of yourself are working, which parts need a vacation. The body? The mind? Your emotions?

Who Should Rest?[1]

THIS BLOG POST IS A CONTINUATION of the entry on "Taking Care of Oneself" (p. 34). In that post I had the illumination that there is a difference between "Me" and "I"—that "I" have to take care of "Me."

Today is a Sabbath, and the Jewish religion prescribes a day of rest. For Christians, it is Sunday. For Moslems, it is Friday. I do not know what it is for other religions, but I believe most prescribe a day of rest.

Rest for whom? Me?

That means I should fast one day a week.

As I said in "Taking Care of Oneself," there are multiple components that comprise "Me." This means that all those components have to rest. Not just my hands and feet from working, or my head from processing information. How about my intestines? My heart? And my emotions? All the components that comprise Me.

For instance, I should give my "food-processing machinery" a rest. That means I should fast one day a week. (It is not strange that one day a week of fasting and only drinking water is prescribed for good health.)

It is not only my mind and body that should not be working non-stop. I should also give rest to my emotions: no problem solving one day a week, and any stress is prohibited.

Obviously, I cannot give rest to my heart but I can help it from having to work hard, which happens when I have emotional problems to deal with or when anxiety attacks take it over. It would be a good idea not to

1. Adizes Insights, November 2012.

exercise one day a week, to give my whole body a rest. Relax one day a week. Give the "I" in you rest too.

Now who is this "I" who will be the focus of this day of rest? Who is the "I" as different from the components that comprise the Me?

It is my spirit. By stopping mind, body, and emotions from taking all the energy, the spirit can receive all my attention. That is why religions prescribe going to a house of prayer on the day of rest: to integrate with something bigger, larger, and absolute, something beyond oneself.

If you are not a follower of institutional religion, what should you do? Have long meditations one day a week. Or go for a hike to experience nature in all its beauty. Rediscover God. Let yourself feel free to be part of something absolute and all-encompassing. Let your spirit be the focus of your existence one day a week. The rest of the week is for the other components of Me.

What happens if you do not have that day "to find yourself," to relax the Me and focus on I? Time flies and you will feel lost. All at once, you are old and wonder what happened, where did time go? What happened to you? Who are you really?

Sad but not hopeless.

Wishing all "YOUs" a periodic rest while alive. Do not wait till you are six feet under....

PART II

❈

RELATIONSHIPS

What Is the Biggest Asset in a Marriage?[1]

IN MY BLOG POST "What is a 'Real' Asset?" July 12, 2013 I quoted David Tice, professor at University of California, Berkeley, who said that the most valuable asset a company has is what it cannot sell. And I totally agreed. Among other things, I believed it reinforced my theory that the most important asset of a company is its culture of Mutual Trust and Respect.

This phrasing—the most valuable asset is "what you cannot sell" can be used to analyze individuals' system of values…Those are not saleable.

It occurred to me that it can apply to a marriage, too.

Why get married? Some people, especially women, marry because the clock is ticking and they want to have children. So a man is a (not necessary but convenient) tool for reaching that goal.

Some marry because they are sexually attracted and want to have a monopoly over their sexual interest.

And some decide to marry because they are lonely now, or are afraid of being lonely when they are old.

Another reason of course is to marry for financial security; find someone who can be a provider.

These are all the wrong reasons if we use the formula "what cannot be sold." Because what cannot be sold can be bought.

You can "buy" your biological children, you do not need to be married for that. Just go to a reproduction center and acquire someone's sperm.

1. Adizes Insights, January 2014.

Marrying for sexual gratification is the most expensive alternative. Sex is easy to buy.

And financial security can be purchased, too.

Marrying because one is lonely is also an expensive alternative. Being alone is easy to solve now or in old age. Go to an old age home and get a nurse.

So why be married?

What is it you cannot "buy?"

It is *love*.

Love cannot be bought or sold. Affection, attention, sex—they all are available on the market, all can be bought and sold. But that feeling of deep, real, honest affiliation, of real belonging, cannot be bought. It is not sold anywhere. There is no potion that can do it. Even God cannot give it to you. God does not say "love your parents." It's impossible to order that. God says "honor your parents."

Love is not available from the outside. It has to be available from the inside, and it is the most important quality in a relationship called marriage. It is the most valuable asset.

Everything else, at best, is a passing reason. The kids grow up and leave the house. Money comes and goes. Friends scatter around the globe. What is left at the end of the day? Why be married if there is no more love? Pure love. True love.

And how do we know if it is pure, honest love?

Remove from your head all the other reasons why you are married to your spouse. If you had no children (and no pets you were attached to) and you were broke, or your spouse went broke and stopped being a provider, and there were people to take care of you like a maid or a nurse, would you still be married? If all the reasons disappear, what is left?

All the other reasons for being or getting married are based on *fear*. Marriage should not be a response to fear. It can and should be only entered into because of *love*. Only *love*.

Think of it: Love applies to children, too. Why have children? In developing countries, they are a source of income for the family. Or they are the insurance that someone will be a provider and caretaker in old age.

These are also reasons based on fear. Unfortunately fear is a reality—a completely rational one—within a developing country. But fear is not a reasonable response for a man or woman in a developed country. Not with health insurance and an available retirement system.

As for companionship, it is becoming more and more sporadic. In to-day's open-borders world, especially in the USA, kids scatter all over the globe, so that form of companionship is limited to periodic Skype calls.

All the other reasons for being or getting married are based on fear.

So why have kids? Because they are the expression of your love with your spouse. Because you cannot help it. It is an urge driven by love. (Psychologists say it is a need to reproduce and secure our human continuity. I challenge that. There are too many of us already....)

Is it not sad when kids are conceived out of hate or pure sexual intercourse without love?

So love it is. It is what cannot be sold or bought. But it can be destroyed in a flash. In a second of rage, disappointment, or reality testing.

You know the value of the most important things in life not by their existence but by their absence.

You do not know the worth of love, health or democracy until they are absent.

Wishing you love in your life.

EXPRESSIONS OF LOVE[1]

THERE ARE BOOKS on "the language of love" that claim different people expect love to be expressed differently. Some prefer being touched. Others expect more time to be spent together and others want presents as an expression of love.

It seems to me that there is another differentiation: Men and women interpret love differently. Not only do their interpretations of love differ, but so too do their expectations about how love should be expressed within their relationship. And that often becomes one of the sources of conflict within a marriage.

Both men and women want and expect love, but the language of love for men is often different from the language of women, and that is the insight of today. (Of course we all recognize that some men have a strong feminine side, some women a dominant masculine makeup, and that people act in accordance with their personality, rather than a gender stereotype. Thus, in this insight the terms *man* and *woman* should not be taken literally.)

I said in the July 2013 blog post titled "Searching for God" that love is total integration, which means mutual trust and respect. You cannot love someone you do not respect, nor trust.

I now realize that was a masculine way of expressing love. Those with masculine energy, for the most part men, desire from their female partners love expressed in respect and trust: *Just show you respect me and trust me as a husband, as a provider, as a father—whatever I am supposed to do.* That is paramount.

Those with feminine energy, for the most part women, want respect and trust too, but their focus or emphasis is on actions that are addressed to

1. Adizes Insights, August 2013.

feelings. They seem to be saying, directly or indirectly: *I want you to take some time and demonstrate that you care about me, that you value me, that you want to hug me.*

Men also want to be hugged, but in moderation, whereas women hope that expressions of love will be constant and overflowing.

A woman bringing flowers to a man does not generate the same response (nor the same feeling of love and gratitude) as a man bringing flowers to a woman.

A man might say: Buy me a shirt or a jacket but do not overdo it. Women love men to overdo it for them.

> *Express love the way the other person wants to be loved.*

Women who show love by hugging and kissing, but then criticize a man tend to miss the target. He will feel disrespected, and thus not loved, even though he is hugged.

What is the moral of the story, of this insight?

Do not express love the way you want to be loved. Express love the way the other person wants to be loved.

(In managerial terms: Have a marketing orientation, not a production orientation; that is, focus on the client's needs.)

I observed recently that this insight has validity for how I behave with my grandchildren. My granddaughter loves to be hugged. My grandson runs away when I overdo it.

We are different. And we have to learn how to treat and love each other differently.

Another moral, I dare to say, is that over many centuries women have successfully indoctrinated men. They have made it perfectly clear just how they expect and wish to receive expressions of love: a thoughtful gift on a birthday; a romantic surprise on an anniversary; an impulsive and spontaneous gesture of intimacy on a commonplace weekend. And they express hurt feelings if men forget an anniversary or, God forbid, a birthday.

We men, however, have failed abysmally to effectively communicate to our partners that we want to be loved more with respect and trust than with a gift of flowers and hugging. It is time we did something about that. With women taking a stronger and stronger lead in relationships, the sex wars are more intense then ever. Trust and respect are tested to the limit and impact adversely how men feel loved.

What Women and Men Want[1]

"WOMEN WANT LOVE. Men want respect."

I do not remember where I read this, but it stuck in my mind and I have been reflecting on it ever since. What do you think?

Now, please note: I do not support the idea that women do *not* want respect. It is a question of priorities. Women want, first and above all, love; then they want respect. Men want respect first, *then* love.

I have observed that when too much love is showered on men, they feel suffocated. On the other hand, the more love you show women, the more they flourish. Latin lovers use this knowledge as a seduction strategy.

And what does "love" mean?

I once read that there are three ways to express love: to give possessions; to dedicate time and attention; and to touch.

A woman who does not get touched or made love to frequently, who gets little attention and material protection, will not feel loved.

Men want respect, and what does "respect" mean? Appreciation for their achievements, no matter how large or how miniscule those achievements are.

We are living in a transitional era, in which women and men are exchanging power positions: Women are becoming dominant and men subordinate.

In this transition, both women and men suffer. Women still want the love that they always needed, but now they also want the respect that men have had.

1. Adizes Insights, January 2011.

Men are left wondering how to adjust to the new reality in which they do not get the respect they need and also have difficulties subordinating themselves to women, who are demanding more and more power.

Women are becoming dominant and men subordinate.

I recognize the possibility that this power struggle might be a generational issue rather than a gender issue. Maybe the younger generations have found a way to balance power. But it remains to be seen whether women's need for a strong man, which seems to be embedded in them, is really an issue of the past.

Maintaining a Marriage[1]

E NTROPY IS NATURAL, caused by change.
With change, things fall apart. Ruin sets in.

Build the most beautiful garden money can buy. Do not maintain it, and it will be destroyed over time, overflowing with weeds.

Do not maintain your car. The most expensive, best car money can buy. Do not drive it. Do nothing to it. After, say, two years, it will not start.

You must "maintain" everything that is subject to change if you want it to function. Your home. Your car. Your garden. And, yes, your company and your marriage.

The prescription for reinvigorating your company you can find in my lectures and books: Redesign your organizational structure periodically. Realign the rewards systems. Redefine your mission. Adapt your information systems to new realities, and do it all proactively. Do not wait until there is a crisis. Review your organizational structure every year, preferably on the anniversary of your last structural change or renewal. It would be wise to review your staffing decisions thereafter; and your information needs, and flows, as well.

Adopt the same procedure with your car. Take it to the garage for maintenance every 6000 miles. Do not procrastinate and bring it to your mechanic only when it is broken or fails to operate smoothly.

But how about a marriage? What does it mean to maintain a marriage, and to do so proactively?

If you do nothing, it will almost inevitably break down. You do not have to destroy it. It will dissolve by itself…because of change.

1. Adizes Insights, June 2013.

A friend of mine recently was shaken. His wife wanted a divorce. "I do not know why she wants a divorce," he said. "I didn't do anything!"

Yes, you have to do something. You have to maintain your marriage.

What does it mean to "maintain" a marriage? I just got the insight talking to one of my clients.

Honeymoon? I was shocked. We were scheduling my visits to his company. I schedule them a year in advance. When I suggested a certain date he said he could not make those dates because he was on his honeymoon.

Honeymoon? I was shocked. When was he planning to divorce his wife? We had just been together for dinner the other evening. Now he was planning to remarry and embark on a honeymoon?

He saw the surprise on my face and, with a smile, calmed me down.

"It is with the same wife. On the anniversary of our marriage every year we have a fresh, new honeymoon. Because," and here is where the tires hit the road, "one honeymoon is not enough for a lifetime of marriage."

Aha! Once a year on your wedding anniversary, go off on a new honeymoon. No children. No one else. Just the two of you. Select the most romantic place you know. An old one that the two of you go back to, or a new one you both want to explore.

Moreover, if you have a rocky marriage, very stressful for whatever reason, take one long weekend away from home, away from stress, from work, from the kids. Go somewhere and be together. Slow down. Do nothing. Just relate to each other and agree that it is forbidden to solve any problems during that long weekend.

Just be with each other. "Replenish the batteries."

Not only your marriage needs maintenance. Your body needs it too. And your mind. For the body, spas are rejuvenating. For the mind, meditation is freeing.

The more you run, the more maintenance you might need.

THE INSTITUTION OF MARRIAGE[1]

FIRST OF ALL, notice that marriage is considered an "institution." It is not called an "arrangement" or just a "system" or an "organization." It is an "institution."

What does the word "institution" mean? It means that there is (A) (from the PAEI code, for the uninitiated) to be followed and respected.

(A) means rules of conduct: who does what, when, how, etc.

That is how the institution of marriage was run for generations: There were rules of conduct transmitted from one generation to the other, culturally, as to what is the role of the mother, that of the father, that of the first born, and that of the last born, and even the role of the grandparents.

Take me, for instance. I come from a traditional Sephardic culture. My grandmother knew perfectly well what her role was. It was clearly homemaking, making a house into a home, raising children and taking care of her husband to the point that she would eat before he would get home so that she would be available to serve him when he ate. Yes, serve. I use this word consciously. She did not rebel against it to the best of my memory. She was proud of the quality of life she established at home, the quality and behavior of the children, and the happiness of her husband.

The husband, in turn, was responsible for bringing the money to the house and for fighting the world out there, so the family would have the resources to survive. He was the breadwinner. He was happy if she was happy. Simple. And the world of my grandparents was simple.

Everyone in the family had a "measurable" performance indicator, or

1. Adizes Insights, March 2013.

KPI. The mother would be appraised by how well the children performed at school and how well behaved they were, the quality of the cooking, and the cleanliness and order that existed in the house. The table, with all the food she cooked, and the children were her portfolio, presented to the family for evaluation.

The father was appraised by how good he was as a provider and as a backup system to discipline the children when the mother failed to get the desired behavior.

The grandparents were the (I), monitoring that the husband, the wife, and anyone else in the extended family, did not deviate from the norm. They were the judges of the adequacy of behavior and, in a sense, the psychotherapists.

This was how my home was run when my grandparents were alive. This is how I remember the institution of marriage, of having a family—but that was over seventy years ago.

One can still find such marriages in very traditional or religious families in the Jewish community or in developing countries. (I just came back from India, where I stayed with an Indian family for a week. That household was run this way, too.)

It has all changed in the developed world. With two-career families, with grandparents living far away, with the advance of ready-made food and the culture of eating out, the rituals, the rules of behavior, the expectations, everything has changed.

Now who is responsible for what, and who is expected to do what, is all up for grabs. The (A) has gone to hell and many marriages feel like hell too.

What to do?

There are attempts to find a solution. One of them that seems the most prevalent is to substitute the (A) with (I): We need to love each other, and by understanding each other and loving each other we will find a solution to all our problems and disagreements.

Pardon me, but that does not work, and the rate of divorces supports my opinion. Love is fickle. It comes and goes. (I) without threshold (A) is very vulnerable. It cannot stand the turbulences of life.

It seems that it is necessary for each couple to custom create the (A); it is not delivered by tradition anymore.

That means that before getting married the couple in love should take the time to cool their heads and sit down and write—yes, write down—their agreement on everything: What are the values they hold dear and that will not be violated? Is it going to be an open marriage or not? How many kids are they aiming to have? Who is the main breadwinner? Will either one of them stay at home to raise the children, and if they are raised by a nanny who will supervise her? Where will they live and what size of house are they aiming for? Who washes dishes and who takes care of family accounting? Who drives the kids to school, etc. Even how many times, minimum, both parties agree to have sex in a week, or month, or whatever.

Everything should be discussed openly so that neither one of the parties later on starts resenting living in an institution in which he or she did not agree to the rules of conduct.

They should discuss and agree on all the details that, if not articulated upfront, can be a source of hard feelings later on.

This document should be a living document, which means it should be up for review on a predetermined date annually, rather than waiting until there is a crisis to review it. Needs change. Expectations change. So the document might need to change too. But it should be on predetermined date and thus be handled proactively.

A marriage needs a lot of (I), granted, otherwise why be married—and the more (I) the less (A) will it need. But having no (A) and relying only on (I) is a mistake that will cost both parties dearly when they get divorced, and divorces are not cheap financially or emotionally.

If the couple does not get divorced both parties will be robbed of energy by having endless arguments or hard feelings because their expectations of what the other should or should not do are not being met.

"But it is very unromantic to have such a meeting and such a discussion, and then a written document," one person told me. My response: Do all your divorcing before getting married.

And even then, this is not all you need for a sustainable marriage. You still need good luck and lots of it.

Lifecycle of a Marriage[1]

I WAS RECENTLY TALKING to a young lady at the health center at which I'm staying. She is contemplating marriage, but has doubts. It's not that she doesn't love her future husband. Rather, she is scared of the institution called marriage.

"So many get divorced," she says. "Apparently a good marriage has a time span of, at maximum, fifteen years."

This made me think.

Here is what I said to her: You are right, many people get divorced, but only if the behavior between the spouses does not change over time.

The reasons people want to be married to each other change with time. Marriages have a lifecycle, and if both parties do not change how they relate to each other throughout its course, the marriage will dissolve emotionally and, in some cases, legally.

When a couple first marries they are typically doing so because of physical attraction and "love that cannot be explained." Then, when and if a child is born, this relationship has to change: Now they need each other to share the responsibility of raising children and supporting each other.

When those children are out of the nest and the two are left alone and retired, the needs change again. Now they need in each other a real friend with whom to age graciously, to go places together, and to learn new things together.

It is not the same "marriage" for the length of the lifecycle of a marriage.

People who do not change "grow apart," which leads to divorce legally

1. Adizes Insights, December 2011.

or emotionally; by emotionally I mean they are "divorced" behaviorally while married legally.

Here are examples of failed transitions:

I have known people who get married but their behavior continues as if they were single. Obviously it does not work.

A successful marriage, like any organization, has a lifecycle.

When a child is born if the husband continues to have demands as if nothing has changed it is not good either.

When the children are out of the nest, if one spouse continues to brood about loneliness and feel depressed for having lost the role of being a mother or father, it is not good either.

When looking at a potential spouse, I said to the young woman at the health center, look at how that person would be for the long run. Do not make a decision just because you are infatuated now.

Okay, you are in love *now*, but how will it be for you when you have a house to take care of, and a mortgage, and various obligations that need to be met as a couple, as a family?

When the children are born how will your spouse be as a parent? (Look at how their parents raised them; apples do not fall far from the tree.)

How do you believe your spouse will be as a friend when you are alone and retired? Can you imagine that? (Again, look to the parents....)

A successful marriage, like any organization, has a lifecycle. Our style has to change as the marriage moves along the lifecycle. If one or both of the spouses do not change, it will bring tension and stress to the marriage, and maybe divorce too.

> Author's note: I am aware that this blog oversimplifies the causes of a successful marriage or of a divorce. There are many more factors to consider. In this post, I wanted to highlight one factor out of many: the need to change as the marriage goes through its lifecycle.

Marriage As a School[1]

THIS SPECIFIC BLOG is probably going to get me in hot water. Again. And I have to remind myself that I have to be what I am with no fear or pretentions. Just be and learn from criticism. I mean constructive criticism.

So, here it is.

One grows a lot in marriage. Through a lot of conflicts. Through resolving a lot of interpersonal stylistic issues.

One learns to be patient. To wait and wait and wait for your wife to do all her makeup and be ready to leave the house. Or for your husband to stop watching that football game.

One learns tolerance, and to sometimes accept what one does not like because the other person does like it.

You learn to pretend, too. If you are asked by your spouse to give feedback on how she looks in her dress, you better tell her that she looks fabulous although you are not too excited with the color of the jumper she is testing out.

Why pretend? Because she is not asking for your opinion, she is asking for reinforcement that she made the right decision. If you tell her what you truly think, you might get criticized that you have no taste and no idea what is right or wrong. The same applies to a woman when a man asks her what she thinks of his new car.

You learn to let your husband drive in circles refusing to listen to your instructions, although you know the direction perfectly well. Patience. Tolerance. Space.

1.Adizes Insights, July 2014.

You learn to take it when the spouse gets angry. To not react. Swallow your pride and deal with the issue when "the storm is over."

You learn too how to deal with a grown up man who at times behaves in a childish manner; all he cares for is food, drink, sex, and comfort.

These are the people that never grow up. One learns to deal with a hurt masculine ego, how to deal with it in a way that does not hurt the ego although it needs to get hurt.

Yes, marriage is an ongoing class, and you are being tested in real time, all the time.

It is an ongoing class with stern teachers. Each one is a teacher to the other. We are students and teachers at the same time. Tough.

Some do not make it. They flunk the tests and repeat the class over and over again. I mean remarry multiple times looking for the perfect spouse, which obviously does not exist. It is tantamount to looking for a university where you learn nothing. Or they drop the class or the "marriage university" all together and get divorced. Some do not enroll in this university to start with. They never marry.

These are the people who never grow up. Never mature and never understand that life is ongoing learning, and real learning comes with the pain of solving real issues in real time with real people.

Is there a time when one graduates, and there is no more pain, i.e., no more learning? I do not think so.

You can graduate from a class, i.e., you have learned your lesson on a certain topic, but school continues and along the way you get enrolled, whether you like it or not, in a new class. New conflict. New problems.

You graduate from this school when the classes are review classes: You learned whatever there was to learn, and now you just have review sessions; you have dealt with the issues before. Learned your lesson, learned what can and cannot be changed, and learned to live with what cannot be changed.

But not all people suffer. There are those who enjoy the learning. The growing. They love to learn and to teach, and love to enrich each other.

When does that happen? When there is mutual trust and respect in a marriage. When that happens, disagreements and conflicts are an opportunity to learn, enrich, and support each other. Spouses do not take the conflict personally. They realize here is another opportunity for me grow up and learn something new.

Without mutual trust and respect, learning is painful and feels like a punishment.

WHAT MAKES A PERSON ATTRACTIVE?[1]

IF YOU ASK A MAN what makes a person attractive, you will get different answers than if you ask a woman.

Men, as I understand, usually focus on physical attributes: the legs, the breasts, etc. Women tend to focus on the brain and on a man's ability to support and defend, etc.

I have another idea, which I hope both sexes can agree on. (And if you predict that it has something to do with integration, you're right.)

When a person has it "all together"—i.e., is integrated—none of their energy is wasted. This person *exudes* energy, while a person who is "falling apart" *takes* energy from the people around him or her.

Who is attractive? Those who give you energy, not take energy from you.

People who "have it together" are attractive. Those who are "falling apart" are not.

Years ago, I hired as my assistant a young woman I felt was rather plain and unattractive. On purpose. I assumed that attractive women would distract me from work.

We started working together, and over time I found her to be smart, intelligent, easily receiving and granting respect and trust. I frequently sought her opinion, and respected it: I found her opinions very valuable. I learned a lot. And I trusted her word. If she said something would be done, it *was* done.

Over time, I stopped noticing her crooked nose or protruding chin. I now thought she was beautiful, and I was hopelessly attracted to her.

1. Adizes Insights, June 2011.

Unfortunately for me, she was in a committed relationship.

On the other hand, I remember dating a woman who was knockout gorgeous. She had a perfect figure, a face that was hypnotically lovely. She was also well educated and came from a respected family. But I lost interest in her within weeks. My endless enthusiasm ended up in endless disappointment.

What happened?

I now thought she was beautiful, and I was hopelessly attracted to her.

She had no self-trust or self-respect. She sure was not "together." And because of that, I believe, she had no trust or respect for others—in this case, for me.

She could not make a decision on her own, and acted totally dependent on me. But when I did make a decision, she did not trust that decision. We had endless debates about what to do and who was right.

This kind of person, often called a "high-maintenance person," has no self-respect and no self-trust. She is not "together," not integrated. As a result, a lot of her energy is wasted between her ears. She usually looks tired—*emotionally* tired, not necessarily physically tired. She might tell you in a debate: "Never mind," or "Fine," but I have come to learn that this only means the debate is being postponed, not actually resolved.

Although such people can be physically stunning, they often become unattractive to the people they are with, despite being intelligent, highly educated, powerful, and successful.

Being attractive depends on the flow of personal energy, which is a function of physical, emotional, and spiritual integration—in other words, being healthy in body, mind, and spirit.

The Discomfort
of Being Rich[1]

I HAVE NOTICED an interesting phenomenon with older rich people, especially those who made their fortune with their own hands.

They develop a certain suspicion: Are they really loved independently of their wealth or are they loved because of their wealth? Do people seek their company because they want a donation to a cause? Are their relatives, even their own children, nice to them because they want to be remembered well in the will, or are they genuinely loving?

Rich people can be suspicious.

Some of them even hide their wealth for fear that it will lead to the wrong friendships. Or they stick to friends who are as rich as they are so they do not have to suspect them.

How many of us would like to be wealthy but are not aware that wealth carries with it a price? That it impacts the nature of relationships?

We all want to be loved. I think it is the most basic need of any organic system. Even plants flourish more when shown love, when spoken to with gentleness. Pets for sure react to love. So do people. When we doubt whether love is genuine we are in pain, are we not?

So, being rich is not such a blessing. One is blessed with materialistic benefits but is saddled with suspicions about love, which is the most valuable asset there is. One wonders if the love shown is true love or a love based on selfish interests.

This explains to me why poor families are stronger families. They show much more love and respect for each other than rich families.

1. Adizes Insights, July 2013.

And I wonder who is "richer?" The one with the money or the one with love?

Interesting that everything comes in pairs. No benefits without costs. And apparently all costs have their benefits. We just need to recognize them.

Why Being Creative
Is Dangerous[1]

I MEAN DANGEROUS to your personal life, to intimacy. Study the biographies of great artists in all fields. Many have had more than one divorce. Some never marry. Or never remarry. Some live a bohemian life, moving from one relationship to another without any depth or intimacy. Some find love in the bosom of prostitutes.

The same appears to be true for great entrepreneurs or innovators. The common denominator being creativity.

Now, why are being creative and being intimate incompatible?

Because energy is fixed. Being creative requires lots and lots of energy. Little, if any, is left for interpersonal relations. Marriage requires work. Intimacy is not free; it takes energy to maintain it.

This illumination explains to me why Buddha had to leave his family, his wife, children, everything, to seek enlightenment. It is apparently not easy to be enlightened, trying to maintain peaceful relations with a spouse.

A big part of the calories we consume is for the brain to function, and when we are creative we require a great many extra calories. We need energy. It is not strange that after a day of creating anything, not just artistic creations but anything new, we are exhausted, more tired than if we had been digging ditches.

To be creative as an artist, as an entrepreneur, as an innovator, or as a political leader, you need a supportive, understanding, and non-demanding spouse. You need peace and quiet, and the least stressful environment.

1. Adizes Insights, October 2013.

It is not surprising that artists are accused of being narcissistic. They need total support, and they insist the world around them conform to their wishes, so that all their energy can be dedicated to their creative pursuits…whatever form those pursuits may take.

A big part of the calories we consume is for the brain to function.

Not many spouses are willing to put up with it.

So the price of being creative—as a leader, an entrepreneur, or a true, fine artist—may be a high personal cost. It often leads to problems with intimacy, and to a narrowing down of friendships.

Apparently nothing comes free. To create something new, you have to give up something else.

On Father's Day[1]

"Honor your father and your mother, so that you may live long in the land the Lord your God is giving you" (Exodus 20:12). That is one of the Ten Commandments.

Why is this commandment so important that it comes fifth? That's pretty high on the totem pole, even before "You shall not murder," which comes sixth. As a matter of fact, honoring your parents is the first commandment that deals with the relations between people. The four that precede it concern man's relationship to God.

Why is honoring your parents so important? And what, exactly, does honoring your parents have to do with living longer on earth? How are those two concepts related?

First, why is it so high on the totem pole? I suggest it is because the family is the building block of society. If the family is "broken," crime could result and thus "do not murder" and all other commandments that follow it are the product of having a dysfunctional family. So start by having your family relations in order.

Okay, but why will honoring your parents prolong your life on earth?

Imagine that you are old, feeble, weak, and vulnerable, with no energy to stand up to anything. All you want is some peace in the sunset of your life. But you have none. Your children treat you with disrespect. They interrupt you when you talk. They make fun of you constantly because you forget things. They ignore your special needs, and you have to struggle to deal with them by yourself.

I do not know what you would do, but I would ask the Lord to take me as soon as possible. Life would not be worth living.

1. Adizes Insights, June 2012.

Now, imagine you are that same person, but that in the sunset of your life you are surrounded by respect. Your children are there for you when you need them. They are attentive and they honor you.

You will live longer than in the former case, right?

Okay, then, honoring your parents prolongs their lives, but why will it prolong *your* life?

When you honor your parents, your children are watching. You are modeling the appropriate behavior and helping to ensure that they will honor you when you get older.In that sense, helping your parents live longer will also help you live longer.

But why "honor?" Why not "love?"

Honoring is not related to feeling.

There is always tension between parents and children. That's the way life is. Parents have to make decisions that children, while they are growing up, do not appreciate at the time. There is resentment, sometimes even a strain of hate. And parents are not always happy with their children, either. It is hard work raising them, setting boundaries for their behavior, and helping them find a direction in life.

That kind of stress is normal thus, not even God can instruct us to love our parents all the time.

But God can instruct us to honor. Honoring is not related to feeling. It is related to behaving regardless of how you feel. No one can order you how to feel, but they can order you how to behave.

When you honor somebody, you behave as if you love him or her, and that is what God wants us to do: to behave as if you love, regardless of how you feel. Honoring your parents will have the same results, as far as prolonging their life, as loving them. I suggest to you that love is empty talk anyway unless it is followed with appropriate behavior.

Next question: Why does the commandment say "to honor," rather than "to respect?"

In Hebrew, the word "to honor" is *kabed*, or *kaved* (the B and V are interchangeable). The root of *kaved* is KVD, which means "heavy." When we honor someone, we bend over, we bow our heads, and behave as if something very heavy is on our shoulders. We are recognizing that the other party is a "heavyweight" compared to us.

On the other hand, when we respect someone, we are recognizing that he or she is different from us and has the right to be different.

Recognizing that our parents are different is not what God instructs us to do. God is instructing us to recognize that they are "heavier" than us. (With the internet revolution and high-tech gadgets, I observe that children feel they are "heavier," smarter, more knowledgeable than their parents, and often do not miss making it known...a definite challenge to this commandment.)

Now, should the word in the commandment be translated as "appreciate" rather than "honor?"

No, because "to honor" does not require a specific cause. In other words, you must always honor an older person, particularly your parent, because of who they are, not because of what they have done for you.

The commandment demands the unconditional recognition of your parents, who deserve honor simply for being your parents.

Happy Father's Day to all.

Father–Son Conflicts[1]

I T IS APPARENTLY NEVER TOO LATE to learn something new. And crucial. And I recently learned something which I recognize is just that, crucial.

Although it should not have come as a surprise to me, I was taken aback when I heard how difficult and sometimes debilitating it was to be the son of a very famous or successful person.

Apparently every son wants (and in many instances, needs) to be better than his father. If the father is famous and very successful it sets the bar very, very high for the children. And if they feel incapable of reaching, let alone surpassing, that particular bar it can be debilitating.

At a party not too long ago, really a celebration, I was talking to the son of the honoree, a very famous and renowned figure, someone I have known for many years. Maybe that is why what his son said surprised me. I think it is better if I leave out names and protect the identity of both the father and the son. The young man was telling me how difficult it is to be the offspring of someone so famous.

At first I thought he was speaking in jest. But the tremor in his voice soon made me aware that he was speaking from the heart.

First, he explained, he does not have a father like everyone else. He has to share this father with more than one hundred thousand people, and in turn receives barely any attention. On his father's end, there simply is no time. But that is not all, he confessed. At heart, he often feels like a failure.

A failure? I was disbelieving. He is a youngster of some accomplishment, I pointed this out.

1. Adizes Insights, June 2014.

He waved a hand dismissively.

Whatever his success it was nothing compared to his father's achievements. And thus, he did not feel particularly valued by his father.

Has he told you this, I asked?

No, was his reply. Not in so many words. But his father's standards were very high and his expectations for himself and me, he explained, are high too.

I see that every day, he said. At meals. In quiet conversations. I feel as though I am constantly under the microscope, being evaluated and criticized by him, and it really is quite discouraging.

What made his father so successful was an incredible drive and self-criticism, I realized. Always struggling for more and better. But when those criteria were applied to his son, apparently they destroyed him.

Whatever I do, the son said, there is an invisible standard that my father has created and it is never out of sight. In my mind he seems always to be competing with me. And I can never win.

I could hear the anguish in his voice. And it opened a door for me. I suddenly recognized all of my own missteps as a parent. I am never happy enough with my own achievements and always strive for better and more. That is one of the reasons for my success. But when applied to my sons and daughters, I saw suddenly, it is very hard on them. They have all stretched in ways that still startle me. But my voice could have been quieter; my striving reined in.

My insight: The more famous you are, the more humble a life you should lead...at least as far as your children are concerned. Criticize yourself as much as you want but leave those close to you alone. Close one eye. Keep your success to yourself and do not act at home the way you do at work.

I do not know how children of movie stars manage. But now I understand that some have to be famous stars themselves or they are miserable. Someone told me Gandhi's son committed suicide. I wonder what happened to Einstein's son?

And daughters, I am told, have the same problem with their mothers. Or at least similar ones. And think about it. What about spouses with a very successful partner? How does it impact them in their marriage?

PART III

✳

SELF-
KNOWLEDGE

Awareness, Consciousness, and Conscience[1]

WHAT IS THE DIFFERENCE between awareness, consciousness, and conscience?

I have been wondering about this for quite a while, and the answers I got from the literature I was reading were not satisfactory to me. The literature dealt too much with physical aspects of how our brain functions and presented research on how the brain operates when parts of it are surgically removed, etc.

Let me approach it with my PAEI model.

To be aware, you do not need to process information with the mind. You are aware, for instance, that you are cold, or hungry, or that you need to go to the bathroom.

The reaction to awareness is usually programmed: get a sweater, eat, or go to the bathroom, as the awareness dictates. There are no feelings associated with the activity of being aware or of reacting to it.

I would call this the (PA) level of relating to stimulus. (P) because it is reactive and (A) because the reaction is programmed, predictable. You do not think about what to do. You just do it.

Consciousness is more than awareness. To me it is the understanding of the repercussions of how you react, or do not react, to what you are aware of. For instance, if you do not eat when you are hungry you might have hunger pains. Or if you do not go to the bathroom to relieve yourself when you are aware of the need to release you will be in pain.

In managerial terms, you are aware of being short of cash. You are conscious that if you do not get the cash you need, you might go bankrupt.

1. Adizes Insights, July 2012.

An example from personal life: You are aware that you are traveling too much for work. Are you conscious of the fact that it is destroying your marriage?

One can be unaware. These people are like alcoholics who are in denial: "No, I do not drink too much at all." One can be aware but not conscious, like the drug addict who tells you, "Oh, this drug is not so dangerous. It just got a bad rap!"

Awareness is reactive. Animals are aware. When they get hungry they go search for food.

To be conscious one needs to be proactive. To be proactive one needs to be creative, to imagine what will happen unless one acts now.

Thus, I would attribute consciousness to the (E) role of relating to stimuli.

Now what is conscience?

This is a new level of relating to stimuli.

It is not just being aware of what is happening, nor being conscious of the repercussions of your actions or non-actions. It is the feeling one has of whether your actions are right or wrong. Conscience has to do with values, not with logical deliberation.

Having conscience means having values. Feeling guilty. Having remorse. Or feeling complete, at peace with oneself, for doing or not doing something. That is level (I) of how we relate to stimuli.

And that is what differentiates us humans from animals.

Plants are aware. Some animals are conscious. But only we humans are aware and conscious, and have conscience.

Pet dogs that live long enough with their masters behave as if they have conscience. When doing something that is forbidden they hide or put their tails between their legs, lower their head as if asking forgiveness. I suggest to you that this behavior is not conscience. It is consciousness. From experience they have learned what is a no-no, and now that they have done something bad they are afraid of the repercussions.

Conscience is not learned. It is not based on experience, good or bad. It is embedded in our psyche. We are born with it.

Research shows that babies know right from wrong at a very, very early age.

Conscience is not based on experience. It is like a chip embedded in the software that guides our behavior.

Where does conscience come from? Is it some experience from the past, embedded in our genes? What is it?

When God drives your conscience, it comes from the heart.

I believe it has to do with a higher conscience: God. To me God is the absolute conscience. And since we are made in His image, we carry this connection about what is right and what is wrong when we are conceived, not just born.

Here is a catch, though: Every one of us has a bit of the saint and a bit of the devil in us. As if both the devil and God have created us. Thus, what is right and what is wrong depends on who is running our "software."

Take the killing of a human being. The God in you would feel guilty if you killed someone. Thus, people confess. They cannot keep the secret too long. They have remorse.

But if you are in a time of war, you might feel remorse and feel guilty if you spared the life of an enemy. You need to kill him. That is the devil in action now.

I suggest to you that when God drives your conscience, it comes from the heart. When the devil drives your conscience, like telling you to kill the enemy, it comes from your mind: You tell yourself that you should kill. You should do this or that. You close your heart in order to allow your mind to lead you.

How human we are depends on how much conscience we have and whether it comes from an open heart or from a trained mind.

More on Awareness, Consciousness, and Conscience[1]

I HAVE BEEN THINKING ABOUT THE DIFFERENCES that separate awareness, consciousness, and conscience from one another. And what connects them, as well. Understanding the differences might have repercussions for management training and development.

One way to explain the differences is by focusing on where in the body each occurs.

Awareness is derived from our senses: Our nose makes us aware something smells bad, our skin that it is cold or hot, our ears that a noise is too loud or too soft. However, awareness does not necessarily lead to action. Awareness means you perceive that something has changed. That is all. It is all about getting data from our senses and perceptions.

Consciousness is different. It is linked to the brain. You receive the data provided by awareness and think (process that data in your brain) about what it means: Should I stop eating because the food smells bad? Should I wear a sweater because it is too cold? By moving from awareness to consciousness we move from data to information.

Data are perceived facts; information is having knowledge about what those facts might cause to happen. We extrapolate the repercussions of the data we got. We organize the data into patterns in order to make a decision.

Conscience is something else. It is not processed by the brain. It comes from the heart, where the soul resides. It provides information by comparing some absolute value and what that value directs us to do with the information we have on hand and its meaning.

Awareness is to notice a change in a condition.

1. Adizes Insights, February 2013.

Consciousness is to know the repercussions of the data we are aware of.

Conscience is to understand the meaning and values of what we are conscious of.

A person can be aware and not be conscious. Take children who are aware they are cold, but do not know they will catch a cold if they fail to wear a sweater.

A person can be conscious of his actions but have no conscience. Like a corporate manager who is conscious his organization is polluting the air or water but his conscience does not bother him even though he may realize that men, women, and children will become sick.

It appears to me that awareness is a precondition for consciousness, and consciousness is a precondition for conscience; you cannot be conscious unless you are aware, and you cannot have a conscience unless you are conscious of the meaning of your acts.

I believe all three elements are embedded in us when we are born, but develop in a sequence. Awareness comes first. Then as we grow older we learn to process our perceptions. It is experience that helps us understand the repercussions and formulate our responses. That is how consciousness develops.

In the same way awareness is the first (development) step in business. It starts with training in profit-and-loss statements, with gathering data about turnover of inventory and accounts receivable. It is an awareness (often in outline form) of how the business works.

To act on that data and become conscious, business leaders require experience. Managers and executives obtain it over time and with the assistance of knowledgeable people. With experience they develop consciousness. But not necessarily conscience.

How does conscience develop, and when?

How can we develop conscience in decision-makers so they do not pollute the environment? Not because they will be punished by law, but because their heart forbids it!

We need to activate the heart if we want conscience to guide our behavior.

The problem with our management education is that we train our future managers and leaders to be aware, to understand the intricacies of financial analysis and market research. We also train them to be conscious, to understand what the information means to the health of the organization and what will happen if they act one way or another. We work on their brain and how it processes information. Good. But what about conscience?

We do not develop or nurture conscience. We do not nurture the heart. We do not allow the soul to speak.

We need to activate the heart in our leaders.

The heart is a muscle. The more you use it the more of it you have. And the more you listen to it, the better you hear it.

What we do, I suggest, is just the opposite. All those computer games that count how many people a player killed, and all those TV programs that casually broadcast murders, destroy our conscience. Dampen it. Weaken it.

I have a suggestion. Build into the educational process visits to a hospital where people suffer from lung cancer; trips to areas where animal life is disappearing; tours of ghetto housing complexes. In this way our future business leaders may come to understand in their hearts how their decisions impact the world we live in. Let them see and feel rather than only think and read financial reports.

We need to activate the heart in our leaders if we want them making better decisions. Not only enrich their minds, but nurture their hearts, too. Nurture conscience first and above everything else. It cannot be done by reading books or discussing cases in the classroom. It needs to be experienced.

As corporations are becoming bigger and bigger, more and more powerful, think about it: How dangerous is it for our society if our leaders lack conscience? Society cannot control everything by law. The world would become oppressive. We need leaders who are guided by their hearts and not by fear of government penalties.

I had a client in heavy industry in Brazil. His company was offered a contract to build heavy armaments. He refused, although it would have been very profitable.

I know of MBA students who will not work for a cigarette company. At any price. And we at the Adizes Institute will not consult, and thus help, companies that knowingly destroy our planet.

Let the heart speak. Let the soul be heard.

Dealing with Anger[1]

IT IS A FAD AMONG NEW AGE personal-growth gurus to preach that each of us should go back and revisit childhood, to relearn how it feels to be full of wonder and curiosity, happy, living in the moment.

Why is childhood such a joyful time? Because we are integrated. We have no past to feel guilty about and cannot imagine the future well enough to worry about that, either. Past and future are integrated into the present. We are in the "Mine!" state of mind, because what is, what we want, and what we think should be are one and the same. (For more details on the "Mine!" state of mind, see my book *Mastering Change: The Power of Trust and Respect.*[2]

Our physical, emotional, intellectual, and spiritual lives do not begin as separate entities, either. It is only as we grow and they develop, and the different aspects of our selves evolve at different speeds, that we start to feel disintegrated.

As I have remarked in previous Insights, I believe total integration is love.

Why is that so? Because when you love, you feel yourself to be part and parcel of the object of your love. There are no boundaries between you. You and your love feel like a single entity. The New Age teachers who tell us to return to childhood are, in a sense, telling us to return to being in a state of love.

But it is not only New Age teachers who talk about love. Have you looked at any bumper stickers lately? "I ❤ New York," "I ❤ Las Vegas," "I ❤ my horse," "I ❤ …" Love is everywhere. We encounter the same

1. Adizes Insights, April 2011.

2. Adizes Institute Publications, Santa Barbara, CA, 1992.

message in our synagogues and churches. (I do not know what one hears in a mosque, though.) And those who know how to sell love, or even promise love, can make a flourishing business out of it.

Apparently the most basic need of human life is love.

Babies who are deprived of love, research shows, do not grow to their full potential. And children who do not receive love suffer emotionally in their adult lives. Without love, we die inside.

If this is true, it brings me to an illumination: All we do in life, beyond what we need to do to survive—like searching for food and shelter—is for love. What is our need for appreciation and respect if not a camouflaged need for love? And when we whine and bitch and moan, we are desperately calling out for love.

Apparently the most basic need of human life is love.

Wait a minute, now. If all of this is true, then it has repercussions for how we handle anger. When someone is angry at us, maybe that anger is just the manifestation of his fear of not being loved. Your response, rather than reprimanding and correcting the other person, should be to show your love.

How would you treat a crying baby? Would you punish it for crying? Or would you hug it and love it in order to calm it down? Why not treat our spouses and teenagers the same way?

All interpersonal problems—and maybe personal problems, too—are either caused by the unsuccessful search for love, or are the consequence of being denied love.

I would even go further: I believe crime is a manifestation of a deficiency of love. A crime may simply be a plea for attention—for love. (I am not talking about psychiatric cases; or maybe they too desperately call for love?)

What do they give convicts nowadays to calm them down? Pet dogs, to love and to train. It is said to have a positive impact on the prisoners' outlook, socialization skills, and discipline. Makes sense. The convicts finally have some love in their lives.

In the United States, what do hospitals sometimes bring to a patient's bedside? Dogs, trained to lick the patient's hands and sit still to be petted. Why? Because showing and receiving love heals.

My mother, who had no education but was very intelligent, used to quote a Sephardic expression: "Love conquers all. Love heals."

The correct response to an angry spouse may be love, not anger. Imagine a spouse who starts yelling at you. The usual response would be to yell back. What would happen if you said nothing, just went over and hugged her, just as you would hug a baby?

I admit that as simple as it sounds, it is going to be very difficult to practice. But let us at least try.

Denying Death[1]

MY GOOD FRIEND IVAN GABOR had back surgery. It was done badly enough that he could have sued the surgeon for malpractice. He did not.

When I asked him why, he said: "I do not have much time left to live. Why would I spend the little time I have left in court?"

He did not deny his death. He knew it was coming. Soon. So he spent his life on what counts.

I, on the other hand, am in denial of death.

When my mother was dying, I ran to be next to her during the last days of her life. But, I was not next to her while she was alive.

Why?

I deny death. I do not consider it as a possibility to the degree that it affects my actions. It is as if I assumed that since life was forever, what was the rush? There is time. I will see my mom sooner or later. I rushed to be with her only when there was no more "later." Only when I was told that death was imminent did I spring to action.

If we do not deny death, if we recognize it is coming, our actions will be totally different.

Ask yourself, for instance, if the doctor told you today that you have six months to live, would you do the same thing you were planning to do for the next six months, or would you say, "Stop. I have only six months to live, and I do not want to spend them in court, or doing work I hate, or with a person I cannot stand?"

1. Adizes Insights, May 2013.

Our actions depend on whether we project death as a possibility or not.

I think it is too scary to imagine death. And thus, we direct our actions based on a scenario that projects death as being very, very far off. Far off enough to be ignored.

It is much more convenient to assume we will live forever, that there is time, and there is no pressure to make choices. Just let it be and live life as it comes…

Natural, but not smart.

The saying "life is short" is not a stupid saying. It should be taken seriously. Life is short, and it is not a rehearsal. There is no second show. This is it. So are we "spending our time in court," or are we squeezing the most out of the minutes left being alive?

How important is it to win an argument if we are going to die soon anyway? All at once all those interpersonal fights, ego trips, money chasing…everything is dwarfed if death is at the door.

Maybe that should be a thought that governs our behavior. Maybe by accepting the reality of death—truly accepting it, behaviorally acknowledging it—we will make better choices and derive more peace from our lives.

DUALITY AND ONENESS[1]

I AM INTRIGUED BY THE CONCEPT of duality and oneness. It seems to me that there is no duality. There is only oneness. This has interesting repercussions for diagnosing and solving problems.

Look at the moon. It appears that there is the lighted moon and the dark moon. It is the same moon. The dark side is where the light does not shine.

I suggest that there is no hate-love dichotomy either. Hate is where there is no love. Put love into the relationship and it will diminish hate. Like bringing light to the dark side of the moon.

There is no cold-hot dichotomy either. It is cold because heat is missing.

I also suggest that there is no rich-poor dichotomy.

Are people poor because they do not have money? If so, all we have to do is give them money to become rich?

You may have heard about poor people who won a lottery. For how long were they rich?

Now take a rich person—not one who inherited the money but one who is a self-made man. Take his money away. Does he become poor?

I suggest to you that he is broke, but not poor. He has what it takes to regain his financial footing. Being poor is a frame of mind, not only a bank statement.

This approach has repercussions for policy making, for how we treat poverty.

I was just talking to a prominent and knowledgeable man who was

1. Adizes Insights, April 2013.

recently in Haiti. He says that foreign aid has done damage there. All the food coming in as aid is destroying the indigenous capabilities of people to feed themselves.

So giving fish to a hungry man does not make him full. You need to teach him to fish.

The difference between rich and poor is not how much money one has, but rather it is how one relates to money. The frame of mind is as important as possession of tools and information.

There is no effective-ineffective differentiation.

Take the problem of crime. The dichotomy is crime versus righteous living. If we agree with the hypothesis of oneness, where one side is the same as the other, but without an ingredient, then crime exists because there is no conscience that governs behavior. In that case, I suggest, we should not fight crime by punishment. It is almost as though we fight illegitimate crime with legitimate "crime." Fight fire with fire.

Being poor is a frame of mind, not only a bank statement.

We need to inject what is missing. Crime should be treated by increasing conscience. That is what is missing.

Is it not what Jesus preached: Fight hate with love?

If this theory is true, then there is no God-devil dichotomy either. The devil rules when God is absent. It is one and the same conscious energy. One is the absent mirror of the other. When one force is missing the opposite force will take its place. As if the energy is fixed. When positive energy is missing negative energy will take its place. When air is missing a vacuum will replace it.

The more I think about this concept of oneness the clearer the concept becomes. But its application is still elusive to me.

What do you think?

Pick any opposites. Think about what is missing in one opposite that creates the other. Think about whether adding the missing part will change the phenomenon, like bringing light to a dark moon. Or bringing God to chase away the devil. Think: What would you eliminate to make an effective system ineffective? Or better: What would you add to an ineffective system to make it effective?

More About Duality[1]

A PEASANT WALKS TO THE MARKET holding a rope in his hand. Tied to the end of the rope is a cow. People stop and ask him, "Why are you tied to the cow?"

"I am not tied to the cow," he responds. "The cow is tied to me."

"Well, if you are not tied to the cow, why don't you let go of the rope?"

"I can't. If I drop the rope, I will lose the cow!"

This is a Buddhist parable. What it says is that what we control, controls us.

Often we believe that by controlling something we are buying safety, that we have gained freedom. Why? Presumably because we now control the situation. But just the opposite is also true. The more we control, the more we, in turn, are controlled.

Take the founder of a company who is afraid of losing his business. He is obsessed with the idea of control. He wants to be the master of the situation. But in reality, he has become the slave of what he is trying to master. He cannot let go of the business. He may be the warden of the company, but he is also a prisoner of the company he started.

I remember one day I told someone I own my own business. "Ah," he said, "so you are the master of your destiny."

"No," I said. "I am the slave of my destiny."

Whatever you master you are also its slave. Master and slave come together. They are two sides of the same coin, and if you desire one, you must also accept the reality of the other.

1. Adizes Insights, February 2014.

One who tries to master his life becomes a slave of that effort, while a slave, by totally surrendering to life, becomes the master of his life.

Find a guru. Admire that guru blindly and completely. Accept all his decisions without questioning. Voila, you are free. You no longer have to make any difficult or painful decisions. But look again. You are now a slave of the decisions and wishes of your master. Is that what you want?

Do not try to control anything, and nothing will control you. For whatever you touch, touches you. Whatever you hold tight is holding you tight. If you do not want to be held, let go of whatever you are holding.

Who is the hunter and who the hunted?
Have you ever experienced physical pain? Generally if you fight the pain, it hurts more. If you accept the pain, it hurts less. You hold onto the pain, the pain holds onto you. Let go of the pain and the pain lets go of you.

It is an axiom that applies as well to personal relationships. Lovers who want to control their loved ones are slaves of their love and feel miserable. The pleasure turns into pain. The hope *for* love turns into fear of *losing* love.

Who is free? The one who expects nothing and wants nothing. Free.

To let yourself be free you have to let others be free.

Read this once again and slowly. Very slowly: *To let yourself be free, you have to let others be free first.*

You chase that woman of your dreams, but it is she who catches you. Who is the hunter and who the hunted? It is you. The same person.

Here is another case: Cost and value always come together. There is no value without cost, and every cost has a value.

Yes, every cost has a value. Think about some bad experience you have had. Now rethink what value you gained from it.

Here are some possible examples: A woman is fired from her job. In retrospect, it turns out to be the best thing that happened to her. It led her to start a business of her own and build an empire, which she would not have achieved had that "unfortunate experience" of being fired not occurred.

Or a man goes through the terrible, painful experience of divorce. It was not all that bad though. There were benefits. He has become a wiser and more caring person. He has changed for the better in a way that could not have happened without the divorce. The cost had a value.

The reverse is also true. Usually people do not realize it: Every value has a cost. Think for a moment. You are enormously successful, the beneficiary of an incredible career. Now, analyze what it has cost you. What sacrifices have you had to make?

You want to have value? You must be willing to pay the cost.

If a cost has been imposed on you, stop complaining. Look for the value it has given you.

Life is like that: You cannot have one thing without its opposite attached simultaneously.

If you love endlessly and compulsively you will start to feel resentment towards your loved one. It is almost like the beginning of hate, as if love and hate had come together. You love someone and hate him at the same time.

Most of us are unable to see that opposition, that duality, makes up life. So, start practicing seeing duality: You hate someone. Stop and ask yourself what you also love about them. There must be something.

CAGING THE EGO[1]

E GO, I SUGGEST, cannot be permanently wiped out. It has a life of its own. It is like a phoenix. It needs to be captured and caged repeatedly. Otherwise, it runs your life, because ego is never satisfied. Whatever you give it, it wants more.

The question is: How to capture and cage the ego?

The way for me to capture it is to be aware when it is out free, roaming the world and causing trouble. For me and for others.

I become aware of its presence whenever I use any of the following words: Assume, wish, hope, expect, want, request, demand.

What happens when I *assume*? I take a position that I know something already. I prejudge. I take a position of superiority.

What happens when I *wish*? I start to believe I am in control of the situation although I attribute a very small probability of the outcome I want actually happening.

When I *hope* the probability I attribute to what is hoped for is now higher. Much higher than it was when all I did was wish for something.

When I *expect* the probability I attribute to an event is even greater and I am upset if it fails to occur. I attribute to myself an even higher sense of control. Should I lack that control, disappointment sets in.

Want has even more of a sense of control attributed to it. I want something, and if it is not granted, I am truly upset. It should have been granted.

When I *request* something, my belief in my control goes even higher. And

1. Adizes Insights, March 2013.

when I *demand* I am attributing one-hundred percent probability that I am in control.

Assume, wish, hope, expect, want, request, demand.

> *There is a probability that what you assume, wish for, want, etc., will not happen.*

There is a common denominator to the phenomena from *assume* to *demand*: It is the degree of control the ego believes it has over events.

When we assume, it is a whisper. When we demand, it is a roar.

When we use any of these words, or they start running amok in our head, when we start assuming control, the ego is out of the cage.

Do you have the same experience?

How should we cage the monster? It runs our life if we don't. When what we assume or demand does not happen, we are miserable. Disappointed. Depressed. You name it.

What is the opposite of being in control? To surrender.

All religions—not just the Judeo-Christian religions, but even more the Eastern religions—recommend surrendering to God. Just take yourself out of the equation.

And if you do not believe in God? Then the prescription calls for a surrender to life, which means start believing in probabilities. There is a probability that what you assume, wish for, want, etc., will not happen. So it is best to relax.

We are not fully in control. Life is like a theater play—we just should observe it and enjoy the show. We cannot control it.

Is there a situation where the ego is caged as an example?

Yes, there is. A scientist should not manipulate the data to get predetermined, desired, results of the research. The scientist does not know what the outcome will be until the research is completed. She cannot and should not intervene and bias the outcome. That is how science works.

Honest scientists have to cage their egos and let the truth emerge from the research. Whatever it is. They have to surrender.

How about an artist? Is not art the opposite of science? Not at all. A true, fine, non-commercial artist has to cage the ego, too, and follow his inspiration. Be a vehicle for whatever inspires him. Not try to produce art that will get the highest recognition.

But why should we cage the ego? Because when it is free, it runs our life and is out of control. It has demands, which shift to new ones, bigger and bigger ones, whenever we reach any of its early demands. However, when the ego is caged our true self emerges and we find peace. And a sense of gratitude we otherwise would not have.

LOVE AND LIFE[1]

IN MANY PREVIOUS BLOG POSTS, I have debated what love is, and my conclusion is that it is total integration.

When you feel in love, you feel totally integrated with the object of your love, as if you are one and the same. There are no debates in your head about if and when and why and how. Nothing. You feel complete, whether it is with a person of the other sex, or whether you are in love with your car or home.

That is why some religions say that since God is everywhere and everything, since it is a total integration, God is love.

That is why we are happy when we have love in our life, and the more love the happier we are. We are "together" and no energy is wasted on doubts or questions.

Now what is *life*?

Life is *change*.

Without change, there is no life. Look at anything that is alive and notice that it is changing right there in front of your eyes: children, trees, flowers, horses… you name it. And since your organization, your business, and also your family, is changing in its internal dynamics…guess what? They are alive, too.

What happens in change?

Disintegration.

Why?

Because all living entities are systems. Every system is composed of sub-

1. Adizes Insights, November 2013.

systems. And, those subsystems have their own subsystems, ad infinitum.

When there is change the subsystems do not change in synchronicity. Some change faster than others. You, for instance, could be physically forty years old, intellectually seventy years old because of lots of wisdom-generating experiences you have had in life, emotionally still a teenager, and spiritually maybe not born yet.

Since life is change and change causes disintegration, we can simply conclude that life is a disintegrating force.

Let me repeat for emphasis: *Life* causes disintegration, while *love* causes integration. They are opposite forces.

The more hectic life is the less love you will find.

This is an interesting conclusion, at least for me. It brings me to many insights.

Here is one: If you do not have love in your life, you are falling apart. To fight the difficulties of life is to seek and find and nourish love. Through true, not just ritualistic, religion. By being truly spiritual. By volunteering in your community, loving your community. Loving your country. By loving your job through loving your employment and your colleagues.

Love is the antidote to the pain that life brings by its nature.

The more hectic life is the less love you will find. Show me a city where life is hectic and I will show you people having difficulty finding love in their life.

How does one find and nourish love? By slowing down. Have you ever seen anyone falling in love by chasing a bus or working eighty hours a week? People fall in love on vacation, walking on the beach at sunset, having dinner with mellow music by candlelight. "The devil is in the haste," says Islam. To find love, God, happiness, you must slow down.

Some people do just the opposite, working harder and harder, looking for "success," hoping that it will bring love and happiness. How wrong and misguided. Time to change. And the sooner the better.

THE RELATION OF LOVE AND CHANGE[1]

WHY DO LOVE AND PAIN go together? (Or, as a Serb song says: *"Zar bez suza ima ljubavi?"* "Can there be love without tears?")

Here is a commentary by Hazrat Inayat Khan (the founder of Western Sufism, who lived from 1882 to 1927):

> The effect of love is pain; the love that has no pain is no love. The lover who has not gone through the agonies of love is not a lover; he claims love falsely. … [The thirteenth-century mystical poet] Rumi describes six signs of the lover: deep sigh, mild expression, moist eyes, eating little, speaking little, sleeping little, which all show the sign of pain in love.
>
> —*The Teaching of Hazrat Inayat Khan*, Vol. 5, *Love, Human and Divine*, 4. *The Moral of Love, The Pain of Love*

Why does love give both the loved one and the lover a sense of unending happiness, and at the same time a feeling of deep pain and despair? What is going on?

In previous blog posts and other works, I have claimed that love is the expression of total integration. When we love, we feel completely united with—we feel one with—the object of our love.

That exalted happiness is caused by the feeling of being fully integrated, because integration, instead of expending energy, creates it. We feel more energized when we are integrated, when we are loving or being loved.

Love prolongs life. Hate shortens it. Look at people in love. They look radiant. Younger than their age. And look at people who hate. They look old.

1. Adizes Insights, May 2011.

Now, why do love and pain go together?

The pain happens because total integration cannot be sustained. The reason is inevitable change. And with change inevitably comes disintegration. With disintegration comes pain: Even if the disintegration is temporary, it hurts to feel the joy of integration fade away.

Take the following example: You are with your beloved, walking on a secluded beach at sunset. No interruptions. The two of you are one. But one cannot continue walking on a secluded beach forever. Life, and work, intervene. Sometimes there are unavoidable absences, and one of the lovers might feel neglected. That is when the fear sets in: Is there a threat to our unity? Is this separation forever?

Love prolongs life.
Hate shortens it.

The higher the rate of change, the more threat to the state of total integration that we call love, and the more yearning for love there will be. And naturally, when change is accelerated and unpredictable, the fear of disintegration is at its highest and the search for love at its most intense.

In fact, it is during such periods in history where change is so disruptive and intense that religious revivals occur and new religions are born. That is when people yearn for the eternal love of God, or Jesus, or some other guru.

Another application of the above thesis that love and change are interrelated is the sense of alienation and intense search for love in fast-moving metropolises. If you want to find lonely people, desperate for love, go to any big city where the tempo of life is fast.

People in large cities are more lonely and their need for intimacy and love more intense than people in small villages. Look at bumper stickers on cars in large cities. Lots of them proclaim love for something—"I ❤ NY," " I ❤ my horse," "I ❤ the Yankees"—and it is a big business selling "LOVE" in countries experiencing a high rate of change, selling anything that gives people a sense of integration.

One More Time: On Love[1]

I DEFINE POWER as the capability to punish or reward, and to withhold expected results is a punishment. Which means, power is to grant or withhold expected rewards.

The first conclusion of this definition is that to expect is to give power to whatever or whomever you expect anything from.

Expect less, or nothing, and be free.

Who has power over you?

Whoever you need for anything. How much power that person has over you is determined by how much you need them and how much monopoly they have over what you need.

This explains why love is such an overwhelming experience. We say to our beloved: "I need you. I cannot live without you and you are the only one."

The way to be free is to say, "I do not need you that much and you are not the only one."

What happens then? You have removed the danger of having pain, of being punished, in a sense, when your beloved does not respond as expected. But then you also remove the reward of being in love.

How to avoid having love be a source of pain and still have the joy?

Eric Fromm, the famous psychiatrist, prescribes, "Do not say: 'I love you *because* I need you.' Say: 'I need you *because* I love you.'"

Aha! Do not love because you need someone. That is where love becomes a power game.

1. Adizes Insights, February 2012.

Love independently of need.

Love without depending.

Love should be independent of needs. Love because you love. Period. Nothing to do with needs. Love without question. Without needs. Without limits. Without conditions. Love as a natural, ongoing response to being.

In that case, love is not based on expected rewards, emotional or otherwise. It is what it is. It is like breathing. You do not compute the value of breathing. You just breathe. No one can take it away from you as long as you are alive.

Be loving as a person, period. It is who you are. It is not a response to anything. It is what it is and it is never too late to love…truly.

WHAT IS LOVE ALL ABOUT, ANYWAY?[1]

I ALWAYS THOUGHT THAT LOVE was the opposite of hate. Like white is the opposite of black. Here at the Sahaj Marg Ashram in the Himalayas, I am taught differently.

Chariji, the Master, told me that love is absolute. It is not the opposite of anything, like God is absolute.

"What about the devil?" I asked. "Is not the devil the opposite of God?"

"No. The devil is there when God is absent. Same way, hate is there when love is missing," was his response.

"And why would love be missing?" I asked again.

"Because we are unwilling to love," he replied. "To love is a choice we make.

This conversation made me think. Hate, then, is a choice we make. It is not the opposite of love. It raises its head when love is missing, when we choose not to love. So the way to stop hate is by replacing it with love. Just forbidding or outlawing hate will not work.

But how do you instill love? And, by the way, what is love anyway?

As I have said in many of my writings and lectures, life is give and take. Or, to be more precise, life should be give and take. But is that why you take your little children to the circus? So that you can write in your diary: "I took you children to the circus on such and such day. I gave you something. In the future, I expect you to pay me back and take care of me when I am old and feeble." Is that why you took them? Life is give and take, no?

1. Adizes Insights, June 2011.

God forbid. In the Sephardic tradition to expect from your children is a curse. You give to your children and should expect nothing in return. So why did you take them to the circus? Because you love them and want them to enjoy the show. And what is your reward? Their joy. You are happy because they are happy.

Love is where in the giving is the taking.

So life is give and take, but love is where in the giving is the taking. That is why you should give "with all your heart," without doubting your giving. When it is done from the heart that is when love is expressed. In the Jewish tradition, giving should be anonymous so that you expect nothing in return. That is how you practice love—in the giving itself you found your reward. That is why, in the Buddhist tradition, a Buddhist would say, "Thank you for allowing me to serve you." In his giving he got rewarded.

Next I asked the Master, "How do you instill love?"

"By practicing," he said. "Love is like a muscle. You do not use it, you lose it. Make the choice and start loving, and it will grow. It will become stronger. Love should not be explained. It should be experienced. Practiced."

What Causes Trust, and Its Implications[1]

I THINK I HAVE DISCOVERED the source of respect. It is embedded in the belief that you can benefit from the person disagreeing with you, that there is something to be learned from the disagreement. As if saying: "I will respect your disagreement so long as I believe I can learn from it…and so long as you disagree without becoming disagreeable."

Respect is earned mostly with—and learned from—experience.

The utmost respect occurs when you believe that you can learn from everyone without the need for proof. When your personality is open and curious all the time, you grant respect to everyone.

But what about trust? What makes some people trusting while others react with suspicion?

I think I found an answer.

It depends on whether you believe in a growing or in a fixed—or worse, in a shrinking—pie.

Let me explain.

A belief in a growing pie is the belief that in the future things will be better. There will be more for all of us. So whoever works hard and contributes to the pie will only make it grow, which will benefit everyone. For that reason we will not object too much if one person is exceptionally rewarded.

A belief in a fixed pie is a belief that what is available is limited, so if someone works hard it does not mean the pie will grow. On the contrary, if he works extremely hard, and by doing so manages to secure a bigger piece of the pie, there will be less for the rest of us. Thus, people try to

1. Adizes Insights, February 2014.

undermine the ambitious worker and make it difficult for him to excel, and thus prevent him from taking a larger share of the pie.

In a society with a shrinking-pie belief system, there is an attempt to delegitimize anyone who is entrepreneurial, anyone who might claim a larger piece of the pie for himself. (In the Soviet Union, *entrepreneur* was a synonym for the word *speculant*, and anyone labeled as such was in danger of being sent to a gulag.)

In a growing-pie culture, I can *afford* to trust others and yield to their interests, sacrificing my own. Why? Because of my belief in a growing pie. It leads me to believe that if I sacrifice my interests now, for the benefit of the other party, it will enable his efforts to make the pie grow and I will eventually receive a larger share myself.

There is increasing animosity against those who have made it.

My point is that trust is not some altruistic and pious notion. It is a form of behavior based on a logical belief system. It is in our self-interest to trust and thus encourage others to work hard and find their reward in a larger piece of the pie, because eventually we will receive a bigger piece ourselves.

Let me repeat: It is in our interest to trust.

Here are some musings about how this applies in my analysis of the United States and elsewhere.

American culture has been based, until now, on mutual trust (and respect). I am constantly amazed that the IRS, at least in the past, trusted people to report their income honestly for tax purposes. That does not happen in the countries of my childhood, and now I know why. There the belief system is based on the concept of a fixed pie and everyone is checking on everyone else.

In the US, the culture has been defined by a "the sky is the limit" attitude and if you work hard you can make it big. Moreover, you will be encouraged to do so.

In a fixed-pie culture the opposite occurs. If you are too entrepreneurial and stand out, people resent you. They put sticks in your wheel, trying to derail you. This is typical of old Europe.

I think the belief in a growing-pie system within the United States emerged out of the vast size of this country and its largely unpopulated regions. There was space and opportunity for everyone.

Today the belief in a growing pie is very much alive in Silicon Valley, in high tech, and on Wall Street. But it is less true elsewhere in the nation. We read news accounts of the top one percent getting richer, while the rest of the country feels their lives are becoming meaner and narrower, and that the pie has become fixed—in fact is shrinking—for everyone else. It is creating strong antagonism against well-to-do entrepreneurs. Thus the Occupy Wall Street movement. There is increasing animosity against those who have made it.

With a decline in trust, internal disintegration begins to set in within the body politic and the society at large. The culture becomes narrower, meaner and the political and economic system itself starts to deteriorate.

Quo vadis, America?

WHAT IS TRUTH?[1]

IS THERE "ABSOLUTE TRUTH?" The expected answer is, for sure! Science is all about finding and proving The Truth. But Newtonian physics was the truth only at its time. It is challenged today. So is Einstein's theory of relativity.

So, is there an absolute *sustainable* truth?

I would say the truth is *any concept agreed upon by all humanity at a point in time*. It is sustainable only if and when we can freeze time.

Assume we assembled every human being into one large hall. They debated the meaning of x and came to an agreement. And then time froze. Nothing could change. I would say they found The Truth on that subject.

Since time cannot be frozen, and all humanity cannot debate a subject and arrive at a consensus, there is no absolute truth. Only subjective and temporary truths.

I am always intrigued when a person in a debate claims a monopoly over truth. "That is the truth," he asserts.

We do not know what the truth is. No one knows. We each have our own belief about what constitutes the truth. But that belief can change over time, or when confronted with compelling arguments.

All "truths" are subjective. Absolute truth is a theoretical construct which will never be realized.

If you agree with the above, it should make you more flexible, open to opposite points of view during an argument.

1. Adizes Insights, March 2014.

You cannot and should not sequester yourself in a bunker of self-righteousness.

WHEN NO IS A YES[1]

I HAVE BEEN TALKING TO DR. RON DUSHKIN, an excellent New York doctor of homeopathy. I have known him for ages and we exchange ideas, problems, and advise each other.

Today I told him about my problem saying *no*. Is it that I do not want to offend the other party, or is it that I do not want a confrontation? Or is it that that I have learned to live with pain to survive. So better to accept what other people want, even if I do not want the same.

We are victims, right? But it is not very enjoyable and comfortable to behave this way, because when we do not say no, and yield without really wanting to yield, we resent it. We hold it against the people we believe put us in this situation, in a corner, not able to say no.

We are victims, right?

When we feel victimized, there must be a villain, and the person we did not say no to is the villain.

Many times this designated villain does not even know we consider him or her a villain. They simply believe we said yes by not saying no.

What to do? I asked Ron.

He had a "trick." I liked it and want to share it with you.

Saying no to the other person is equivalent to saying yes to ourselves.

Let me repeat: Any time we say no to something we do not like or want, we are actually saying yes to ourselves, to what we want.

1. Adizes Insights, September 2013.

Some people have difficulty saying no to others because they have difficulty saying yes to themselves. In other words, they do not count. Their needs are not important.

"If I am not for myself, who will be for me" is one of the rules of a Jewish sage.

Why do we consider the interests, wants, and desires of others—our spouse, our children, clients—more important than our own wants and desires?

Ron says when people ask him to do something or to have his time and he does not want to do it, he says: "Sorry, I am not available."

I thought it was not the best answer possible.

I suggested saying: "I wish I could do that, but I have a prior commitment."

Commitment to whom?

To myself, darn it.

I have an appointment with myself. I have a commitment to take care of myself.

Taking care of myself?

I have real pain in my knees. I asked the homeopathic doctor for help. He asked me to close my eyes, hug my hurting knee, and thank my body. Thank it for everything it has done for me.

I realized then how much this body of mine has done for me, taking a terrible beating with my travel schedule, lack of sleep, eating terrible food, pushing it to the limit of its capability…and what have I done for my body? Very little. I take it for granted.

Think about, as an analogy, management and workers: How much have the workers done for the company versus how much the company has done for the workers?

I never think about what my body wants. Until it is in pain. Then I notice it is there.

Oh God, why do you make us old so soon and smart so late….

THE IMPACT OF THE HOLOCAUST[1]

I HAVE JUST FINISHED WRITING MY MEMOIRS, and I have discovered things about myself I was not aware of until I wrote what I wrote...and then read what I wrote.

The Holocaust, which I experienced from the age of four to the age of eight, had a profound influence on my life. I know this seems self-evident, but it has come as a great surprise to me.

I wondered for years why am I so concerned with what is going to happen after I die. Why was I so committed, to the point of being fanatic, about building the Institute, writing as many books as possible, training people in my methodologies to spread them worldwide...and being worried sick about what might happen to it all after I say goodbye forever. I wondered why I persisted, almost obsessively, and still continue to do so, at tremendous cost to my health and to my relationship with my spouse and my children.

Many people accused me of simply striving for money. The truth is I do not even know how much money I have, and I do not even care. I am very modest in my expenses and tastes.

Some have charged me with acting in the service of an overheated ego. That does not feel right either. I do not care how many honorary doctorates I have. It is all for marketing purposes. I am even somewhat embarrassed, rather than gratified, when anyone asks for my autograph.

So what is it that drives me, blindly?

It became clear to me while writing my memoirs.

It is the fear of death.

1. Adizes Insights, November 2013.

Death is final. There is nothing thereafter. When I die, I am not in control of what happens anymore. I will be forgotten. And that to me is the meaning of death…to be forgotten.

Where did I get this fear of death? From the Holocaust. From the concentration camp. From trying to survive hiding in the mountains of Albania. I am so frightened of dying I cannot even allow myself to faint. Maybe I won't wake up….

I am so frightened of dying I cannot even allow myself to faint.

There are more repercussions from that terrible war. I cannot bear to be hungry. I starved in the camp and for many years after, until we finally reached Israel when I was eleven. To be hungry is a terrible experience for me, and my wife knows that if I am hungry she must immediately feed me; otherwise, I become aggressive and very unpleasant to be around.

This difficulty with being hungry impacts my weight. I am told that to lose weight you need to experience some hunger. Each time you are hungry your body is telling you that it needs to use the stored fat; and hunger is a signal that it does not like to reduce the reserves. Since I cannot be hungry, I cannot lose weight easily.

There is more. My memoirs clarified for me why I try to avoid going through Frankfurt airport when I have to change planes in Europe. I sweat passing the immigration booth. It is situated a bit higher than the person asking admission. The immigration official in uniform sits above you and looks down on you. I start sweating as he looks at my picture and then looks at my face. The uniform, the German accent, and the stern look make me very, very uncomfortable. Is it memories of the camp?

For seventy years I have been behaving a certain way, and I did not know why. Now I believe I have an answer. The war imprinted certain experiences on me that control my behavior. Most of it is unconscious.

Who knows how much more of my present behavior is caused by my past.

THE WONDERFUL LIFE OF NOT EXPECTING[1]

I AM IN THE SAHAJ MARG ASHRAM in the Himalayas, trying once again to free myself of the bad habit of expecting, of wishing.

What is going on?

To expect is a prescription for frustration. When you expect something to happen, or when you expect someone to do something, you're suffering from the "this should be and I want it but it is not happening" syndrome: You believe that something *should* happen, you *want* it to happen, and you are probably already frustrated that it *has not* happened.

Express your need, and let it be. The Sahaj Marg meditation teaches you to let go—even to stop wanting, because if we *want* something, we are apparently dissatisfied with what we already have; that is why we want something else. In other words, we do not want what is, which is another source of frustration.

Just let go, *let it be.* Express your need, and let it be. If it is meant to be, it will happen. And if it does not happen, it was not meant to be.

"Hmm," you are probably mumbling to yourself. "Just *let it be*?"

Yes. *Let it be.* Free yourself from the belief that *you* are, or should be, in control of everything that is happening to you or should be happening to you, and thus what you want, you *expect* to happen. Surrender to life, to reality, and become like a feather floating on the waves of life. You will be calmer. You will stop focusing inwardly—on why this or that is not happening. You will stop endlessly processing the same information in your head, managing to accomplish nothing more than deeper and deeper frustration.

1. Adizes Insights, March 2011.

When you stop expecting and wanting, your eyes, instead of focusing inward, "turn around" to notice the world, to smell the roses, to live in the present, to enjoy your life. Your mind is calm because it is no longer so busy fighting reality.

I have been struggling for two years to change my life around to practice this meditation—to stop expecting and start enjoying. It is not easy, especially since I am Jewish, and we Jews notoriously live in our heads. From the moment we wake up until we fall asleep, exhausted, we are busy thinking, expecting, and wanting. It's true that this characteristic makes us very successful in our endeavors, but I believe we pay a huge price: We are miserable. I am certain that more Jews regularly see psychologists or psychiatrists than any other ethnic group.

I am struggling, but I am learning.

Let me give you an example: We are riding in a car to the Himalayas. It is a long ordeal of bumping from one pothole to the next. After about twelve hours of this bouncing around, I have had enough, and I want a hotel room, with a hot shower and a comfortable bed.

Now, imagine that you are *expecting* to get to that hotel. But where is it? You start to become anxious. Why haven't you seen a hotel somewhere along this road? If there aren't any, you start to think that Indians have no entrepreneurial spirit: "Couldn't they even build a hotel on a highly traveled road? Does it take a genius to figure that out?"

Or, let us assume instead that you are more reasonable than that, and do not start criticizing the whole Indian nation because no hotel appears when you want one. You are just tired. What do you feel? You feel sorry for yourself. You sulk like a child.

Now, imagine that you are able to stop yourself from expecting and even stop wanting. You are aware of what you need but you do not expect it nor do you make a scene about how much you want it. Instead, you just relax and enjoy the scenery. And if a hotel should happen to appear along the road, what a wonderful surprise for you to enjoy! You are like a child who receives an unexpected gift: What a wonderful life, full of surprises!

If you happen to be surprised by bad news rather than good news, at least you did not have to suffer through a frustrating and useless loop of thoughts—"This should never have happened… What did I do to deserve this terrible luck? Oh God, why me?"

Let me give you another example of accepting life (and thus death), not fighting it: I have a relative who is EIGHTY-SIX years old. He almost died twice and was revived. I asked him how he feels about those experiences. Is he scared of death?

He feels very well, he said. When death comes, it will come. He is at peace. He felt that he has had a good life so what is there to lament about?

At that point his wife joined in. "And when he passes away, I will go to an old age home," she said. "No use being a burden to my children." This was said in a very peaceful, loving voice: What *is*, *is*. Want nothing, expect nothing. Accept, with love, whatever comes.

But the broader point is not how one should live when dying. This is also about how one should live while living.

Now the doubt: If we can be sanguine in the face of anything life brings, could that destroy our eagerness to succeed in life, to move forward, to have a career? Not at all. Here in the ashram I have met some very successful businessmen, artists, and scientists.

These people still work, produce, and succeed, but they do not act compulsively. They just joyfully let life take its course. They do not try to force life to go in the particular direction they want and expect it to go. Instead, they go with the flow of life, enjoying it as they live it and as they respond to needs and new conditions life offers. Not "forcing" their wishful thinking on life. Just "joining life" as is.

If you can learn to live this way, you will find that more people accept and like you, enjoy you, and even join you. You are not a pushy, angry, frustrated participant in life. You are much more pleasant partner of life, and you might become even more successful in your career and your relationships.

Try it.

On Loving Yourself and Others[1]

T HERE IS A COMMON SAYING: "You cannot love others till you love yourself." It just occurred to me that in order to love others, it is not enough that you love yourself. You have first to allow *others* to love you.

I noticed that people who have difficulty showing love to others also have difficulty accepting love from others. They squirm when someone shows affection. They are uncomfortable with intimacy. When a man or woman tries to get close, they find ways to undermine, or even flee the situation. It is too threatening. Too "hot," and too dangerous. They invent some lame excuse that leads to escape.

This to me looks like "do not show me you love me, so I do not have to reciprocate." The whole experience of a loving relationship here is "outside" the comfort zone.

The result is a most painful dilemma. On the one hand, there is a great desire for love. After all, love is a basic human need that we all have. But at the same time, it is frightening: Desperately wanting… and desperately pushing away what we so deeply desire.

One unfortunate result of this conflict we have is that knowing but not knowing, we edge away and marry the wrong person, a person who cannot show love either. Or we marry someone who loves, but we push him or her away and reject his or her love repeatedly… In both cases, it is to the detriment of having an intimate, caring marriage.

What is the cause of this behavior? In my experience, it is fear. Apparently, in the past to love or to be loved (for some of us) was an exceedingly

1. Adizes Insights, April 2014.

painful experience. Not at all filled with joy, but marked by deep wounds and permanent scars.

Of course, I am not speaking hypothetically.

I am afraid this is my case.

I watched the people I loved the most and who loved me endlessly, my grandparents, taken to the trains of Treblinka never to return. We have a name for it. The Holocaust. But the name itself is distancing. My mother, as a consequence of the Holocaust, had repetitive, periodic heart attacks, which proved not to be real heart attacks, but something that resembled one, but who knew. Not I, a child, who only feared that he would lose his mother as well.

So love for me is very scary. People you love, or who love you, disappear. Better to close your heart to survive. Or treat those who show love with suspicion.

But is this just my problem or the problem of Holocaust survivors in general? And if so, what are the socio-political repercussions of this trauma? Is there an impact on the so-called peace talks Secretary Kerry is trying to mediate now?

PART IV

�֎

SPIRITUALITY

About Life and Death[1]

I WAS VISITING MY MASTER OF SAHAJ MARG in India. He was old and sick, and twice already passed away only to be revived.

I asked him if he was scared of death. I was.

He said, "What is there to be scared of? You cannot be scared of what is inevitable."

He told me of a disciple of his who told him he wanted to live two hundred years.

The idea is not to fear death, but to fear dying while still alive.

"Just imagine," said the Master, "that your wish is granted. When you are a hundred years old you see your children die. When you are hundred and fifty, your grandchildren die…. How do you feel?"

When the disciple realized that, he immediately reversed his wishes. He accepted that he will die when his time comes.

The idea, I think, is not to fear death, but to fear dying while still alive.

How could that happen?

Well, let us define life. I am not referring to breathing, eating, or sleeping. I am referring to life one feels is worth living.

How does it happen?

It happens when you serve something else. Not just yourself.

Look around. Everything exists to serve something else. Look at your body. The heart exists for the rest of the body. And so do the lungs.

1. Adizes Insights, February 2013.

And the liver and kidneys…. The only thing that serves no one else but itself—and thus serves death—is cancer.

To be alive means to be functional. Needed. Serving a cause bigger than yourself.

That is why I will not go to an old age home to wait for death to come and pick me up. That is to be dead while alive. I will work as long as I can breathe, think, create…be needed. I will serve what God has created me to serve. And when we do that don't we feel alive?

There is something else the Master said which I found interesting.

He was looking forward to "dying." I put the word "dying" in quotation marks because we do not die ever. We just change form. The body dies, the spirit lives.

He told me he is eager to realize what is "there."

He had faith. I had fear.

I realized where my fear came from. From the finality of life. Once one removes that fear, death becomes a natural transition.

There is no life-death dichotomy. When we are born we start dying. By the same token, maybe when we die we start reliving. Differently.

IS THERE LIFE AFTER DEATH?[1]

ULTIMATELY, THE MOST EXTREME OPPOSITES MEET. The earth is not flat. If you continually go east, you end up arriving west of where you started.

By the same token, hate and love are not separate. Extreme love is the beginning of resentment and dependency, which can start to feel like hate. And extreme hate can be the beginning of love, when the slightest sign of an opportunity to connect occurs.

Black and white are not really a huge distance from each other. In absolute blackness, you will start to see white spots. And if you look at pure white for a prolonged period of time, you might become blind and see only blackness.

It just occurred to me that if the above is true and universal, it means that life and death are not separate, either. They, too, meet. The beginning of life is the beginning of death. We start dying the moment we are born. If that is true, I wonder, does it mean that death is also the beginning of life?

The first part makes perfect sense to me. When we are born, we are at the beginning of our lives, and that, by definition, is when we start our journey toward death. If we know that statement is correct, then why wouldn't the second part also be correct—that when we die, somehow, a new life starts, too?

I am not suggesting that we are reincarnated as lions or dogs or whatever. I am not claiming that there is life after death. I cannot say I know what it is that I am conjecturing, or what its nature is. But it appears to me that if ultimates do meet, then there is nothing truly ultimate and final.

1. Adizes Insights, February 2012.

How I Found God[1]

L ADIES AND GENTLEMEN, thank you for inviting me to speak about my beliefs and my search for a personal God. I applaud the courage of the organizing committee to invite a management consultant to speak on a subject so far from his body of knowledge.

I am a management consultant, and my specialty is assisting organizations so that they meet their goals more effectively. Quite a few religious organizations, especially the Catholic Church, use my managerial theories and practices to improve how they develop and nurture their congregations…even though the study of religion is not my field of inquiry.

I was not even raised in a religious family. But, I have been a seeker for much of my life, searching for some kind of meaning both in my personal and my professional life. And, in the process, I found my God. In my own way.

I appreciate your willingness to hear my story. Thank you for inviting me to share with you my personal spiritual journey.

I thank you for your trust.

✻ ✻ ✻

One often hears people say, "There is only one God. The God of the Christians, Jews, and Muslims is the same God. We should all live in peace, because we all worship the same God."

One day, during meditation, I wondered whether I agreed with this statement.

The God of the Muslims orders His followers to kill infidels.

1. A speech delivered at the AMICI Convention, an association of Catholic clergy, July 26, 2013.

The Christian God, like Zeus, has a child with a human being.

The Jewish God is jealous and controlling: He orders His believers around, telling them what to do and what not to do, and threatens them with a long list of punishments and disasters if they disobey Him.

I realize I am interpreting the holy books literally, but still, are these three Gods the same?

I do not know, but I do know one thing: None of these Gods strikes a responsive chord in me.

But I do believe in God. Who is my God then, and how did I find Him?

❊ ❊ ❊

And what is love? Two years ago, I joined the Sahaj Marg meditation community. It is based in India, with ashrams worldwide. I joined for a simple reason: I wanted to learn how to meditate. I believed it would be helpful for my work and my state of being. Perhaps it would even bring me some moments of serenity.

I learned how to meditate and came away with much more than I expected.

I found my God.

Let me explain. This meditation starts off in the morning with a prayer that says, in part: "Oh, Master, You are the true goal of human life, for all we are is slaves to wishes that bar our [spiritual] advancement."

Let me analyze the prayer: The "Master" is God. We pray to be united with Him. And what is it we want to be united with? What does God represent?

Love. Total, absolute, unconditional love.

And what is love?

Unity. Integration. Harmony.

The prayer basically says that we all strive to live in a state of love. In harmony. That is the true goal of our existence. But our wishes and desires enslave us, and impede our ability to experience love. In essence, they hold us back from living in harmony, from becoming one with God.

How?

By reinforcing dissatisfaction and unrest.

What are our wishes, desires, and expectations but expressions of unhappiness with what we have right now. We want and expect something else, something absent from our life.

The wishes become a source of disintegration within ourselves. But, it is the expectations that separate us from God.

Why?

Because expectations presume controllability. Expectations assume that we can control events and achieve our desires (which often are mistakenly translated into our needs). We mistakenly believe that power is in our hands.

Death is probably the ultimate example of how this way of thinking fails us. We wish someone we loved had not died. We prayed. Dutifully. But our wishes and prayers were in vain. Our beloved—friend, parent, partner, offspring—died.

We are upset and angry. What has God done to us? Why has He failed us? There is the expectation that our wishes and prayers should have been able to control even life and death!

Many Holocaust survivors denounced God for this reason: How could He countenance such tragedies? Such evil?

When we expect, we want to control God. And this is not the way to find Him.

Wishes, desires, and expectations distance us, undermine our chances of experiencing love and finding and becoming united with God, the ultimate manifestation of love. They enslave us.

Enslave? Yes.

Because wishes, wants, and expectations are inevitably a moving target. They are temporary and ever changing. We may satisfy ourselves for a short period of time. But then a new wish or desire emerges.

It never stops. Thus, the enslavement. We think, "If I had a million dollars, I would be happy." But when that wish is achieved we now desire two million. And when we possess two million dollars, do we not crave five million?

We will stop being slaves when we are free of wanting and wishing and expecting.

Does that mean we should have no wants or wishes or expectations? Such a path would lead to an end of progress.

Of course not. It is important that we continue to strive, that progress not come to a halt.

Let go of the ego. What should drive us is reality, *what is*, rather than our wishes and our ego. When we go shopping, should we shop for the things we want, which have no end, or should we shop for the things we need, which are finite?

When I paint, compose, or create, should I do so because I want fame and riches, or because I need to express myself artistically in order to be who I am?

So?

Let go. Stop wishing and expecting. Surrender to God and His wishes. Accept life as is. Let go of the ego.

Surrendering to God is what makes us free. Believing that we are free to wish, want, and expect is what enslaves us.

One brief example: The rejection of God's will in the form of an unwillingness to surrender—expecting instead to be in control of life—had its manifestation in, among other places, political ideology, namely Communism.

Communists rejected God.

Communists, at the turn of the twentieth century, believed they could plan and control everything. Communists behaved as though they were the twentieth century's replacement for God. They would take control and provide everything. We only needed to respect and obey and surrender to them and their system, in place of God.

It was with a certain irony that some of the leading former Communist writers and thinkers of the last century ultimately became critics of Communism. Arthur Koestler, Ignazio Silone, Richard Wright, and Andre Gide, among others, published a book about their experiences with the Communist political system called *The God That Failed*.

Let me repeat: When we refuse to surrender we consciously, or by default, reject His existence.

The first condition for finding God then is to stop believing that we are in control. Stop expecting. Surrender. Stop wishing, and accept His will.

Okay, to find God, we need to surrender to His will.

Ah, but there is a catch: To find Him, we need to surrender. But in order to surrender, we need to have found Him first. How can we surrender to somebody we have not found yet?

Is this the religious form of Catch-22?

To find Him, we need to surrender.

The solution: In order to find Him, we have to start with the belief that there is God. If we do not believe, we will not seek, and if we do not seek, we will never find Him.

Okay, so, where is God?

※　※　※

I believe that all religions share the same perspective: that God dwells in our heart.

And how do we find Him there?

In meditation, when we calm our mind and surrender to His will, our heart will speak, and we will experience love. We will experience God's presence by finding love in our heart.

Listening to the heart via meditation and experiencing God's presence is not a new discovery. Come to think of it, did not all religions start with a message from God via meditation? Moses went to the mountain and meditated for forty days and nights before he received the Ten Commandments. Jesus meditated too. Buddha found enlightenment meditating under the tree.

I suspect that is how all religions started: with the heart. It is only over time that the heart was replaced by a "manual," that is, the various religious books with instructions interpreting God's will.

Following the manual blindly represents to me the negation of surrendering to God, because in that case we do not listen to our heart anymore. On the contrary, it is as if we took control of our destiny by just assuming that all we need to do is follow the manual.

We need to go back to the essence: Listen to the heart rather than follow the manual blindly, whether it is the Old or the New Testament or the Quran. Read it? Yes. Study it? Yes. But listen to the inner voice of our heart. That is my belief.

❊ ❊ ❊

When we listen to our mind we encounter a debate: pros and cons on any issue. When our heart speaks, there are no questions. No doubts. No disagreements. No cost-benefit analysis. We are complete. There is peace. We experience love. Or, as Guru Dev, a yogi master, says: "When you resist nothing, you automatically experience love." And since love is God, you experience His presence.

Let me now rephrase the Sahaj Marg prayer in its totality and replace God or Master with the word *love*:

"LOVE, you are the true goal of human life, for we are merely slaves to wishes that bar our capability to LOVE. You are the only power that can make us advance spiritually."

Our goal is to love and be loved. Expectations undermine our efforts. And only love can make the difference; only love may change us. And when we experience love and find peace, we are on our way to finding God, because love is God. Total harmony. Total integration. Thus, the One and Only. Thus the power.

❊ ❊ ❊

For a long time, I could not accept this way of thinking and behaving. I was unable to let go and connect with my heart. I trusted my mind. Not my heart.

Listening to the heart to me meant losing control. The mind was different. I believed that I was in control of my mind.

How misguided.

Are we in control of our mind or is it in control of us? Maybe our mind is controlled by wishes implanted by others, by people we want to please. Or by the media that influences us with advertising and promotions and headlines. Or maybe our mind is ruled by an ego we do not control. It is not solely under our control.

How false this world of ours is, the world of non-believers.

When we calm our mind and surrender our ego, give up expectations based on a false sense of control, we are ready to hear the voice emanating from our heart. We will find a kind of peace, a peace of mind. We will then cultivate a sense of gratitude for whatever we have in our life, for better or worse. We will experience love. We will experience God.

Is that all?

No.

* * *

Sitting in a cave or seminary, meditating, listening to our heart, experiencing love, is all well and good. These are all prerequisites for finding God.

But we must also share our love. A song is not a song unless heard. And love is not love unless shared. The more we express our love in action the closer we are connected to God. We have to love others. And not just other human beings.

Do we love the air we breathe? The water we drink? The people we live among? Do we love the sea, the whales, the birds, the forest, the city, the country we live in?

If so, what are we doing about it?

Love needs to be expressed in action: to make a better world. That is what mystic Judaism called *tikun olam*, Hebrew for "improve the world."

To find God, we need to express our love with loving action.

And when we embrace, and are embraced in turn by this way of being, we will find God everywhere. In the smile of a child who has finally been fed. In the whispering of the leaves on a tree that is surviving a natural disaster. In the gratitude of people who are finally feeling safe from war and danger. We will find God everywhere and all the time. Because we opened our heart. Because we listened to our heart and accepted God.

To me, to find God takes more than following rituals and manuals. We need to believe that He exists and be willing to search. We will find Him when we surrender to His will, listen to our heart, find love, and share it by making the world a better place in which to live.

Is that all then?

Not yet.

* * *

I am a management consultant. I am trained to provide something more concrete. What does it mean: "experience love and share it?" What is love? What is the Lord's will? We are supposed to surrender to His will, but what is His will operationally? (Pardon my management consultant term, "operationally.")

What should we do? What is the action we are supposed to take when we share our love?

Some people behave atrociously in the name of "love;" by that I mean, in the name of God. I am a descendant of the Jews of Spain whom the inquisitors tortured and expelled because they refused to convert to Christianity. Is that love? Is that what God wanted?

If God is Love, in order to find Him we need to understand in an active way what it means to love. And comprehend "operationally" what His will is. What is the essence of His being?

Let me try.

Can we agree that love is total integration?

I believe so. That is what happens when we are immersed in creating something we love. We forget everything around us. We are inspired. As Wayne Dyer says, the word inspired comes from *in spirit*. When we create something we love, a painting, a sculpture, when we compose music, or write a book, we are united with the Spirit, with God. We are inspired and become a vehicle of His will. We transmit his wishes. We are totally integrated with our creation.

Now the next question: If love is total integration, what is integration?

It took me forty years to discover what integration is about. I will not bore you with how I figured it out. Let me give you the bottom line: It is mutual trust and respect.

You cannot be integrated with something you do not respect or trust. There is no love without mutual trust and respect.

When is a marriage over? Not when the couple signs the divorce papers. That is the final official act. The marriage is de facto over when there is no more MT&R, when the loss of mutual trust and respect is irreversible.

Now, what is respect and what is trust?

The philosopher Immanuel Kant said that respect is to recognize the sovereignty of the other person to think differently. When we do not accept that a person can think differently, believe differently, we are not respecting his or her sovereign, undeniable right to be different.

When there is mutual respect, there is growth, we learn from each other's differences and grow intellectually and spiritually. When differences are prohibited we find ourselves in a desert. An intellectual and emotional desert. But when they are allowed and nurtured, our surroundings are transformed into a garden, an ecological system in which we are touched and enveloped by synergy.

And when there is *mutual* respect the other party has to appreciate our differences too.

That is not what is happening with some radical religious off-shoots: "Either be like us, believe like us, or we reject you." And in some more extreme religious sects, the litany goes further: We will even torture or kill you unless you behave like us. In my view that is not serving God.

And what is trust?

It is faith that the other person has our interest at heart. That we do not have to fear turning our back to him. That he will protect our back, and, when it is mutual, we will protect his. We share common interests.

When there is mutual trust we reach symbiosis. We help each other. We enrich each other. We seek our common interest. Not self-interest. And not other people's interest at the cost of our own.

Look at my hand: five different fingers together forming a hand. And this is how all saints hold their hand in all icons, straight fingers touching each other. It is like a message they give us. It is a blessing: Be different but still be together.

So, what does it mean to serve God? What is His will?

Respect your fellow man and woman. Appreciate their differences. And at the same time, in spite of their differences, protect their interests.

A businessman who prays dutifully at church every Sunday, but the rest of the week exploits workers and pollutes the air and water—is he serving God? In my formulation the answer is no. With capital letters: NO.

The person who does not go to church but works with homeless people, who helps the destitute, even if he is an atheist, he is serving God without even knowing it.

To summarize, let us try again:

God is love,
Love is total integration, and
Total integration is the existence of absolute mutual trust and respect.

God is in us, in our heart, but it is expressed in how we relate to each other, how we relate to the air and trees, the environment we live in.

The world is a system of interdependencies and God is the essence that drives the system: mutual trust and respect. What makes or breaks the system is the existence or the lack of mutual trust and respect.

MT&R is life. It is love. It is workable unity. It is harmony—different voices singing in unison, complementing each other.

Without mutual trust and respect there is destructive conflict. Disharmony. Social, political, and physical breakdown. When we do not practice MT&R, we are defying God, defying His will. And our world falls apart in more ways than one.

Without self respect and trust we fall apart as individuals. Without mutual trust and respect our marriage falls apart, our country falls apart, our environment collapses. We defy rather than serve God.

Serving God is expressed in the way we behave. And how much love we have is weighed not by intent, but in our action; that is, by respecting differences and seeking common interests.

Hallelujah and may it be His will.

Amen.

ON JESUS CHRIST[1]

I AM JEWISH, and not a member of the Jews for Jesus movement but I believe that Jesus Christ existed.

What is it that I believe?

Throughout the history of mankind, periodically a person is born—man or woman—who genetically, or by upbringing, is more sensitive to values, justice, truth, and integrity. Much more so than even the most sensitive person. They are at the right edge of the distribution curve: the 0.000000000001 percent of the population. (Please do not take the number literally.)

Their (I), from the PAEI code, is the largest of all. They listen to different "music" than normal people and have "a fire in their gut" that compels them to speak what they see and feel. Because they are a deviation from the norm, from the statistical mode, they are not accepted; they are often burned to death (Joan of Arc), or crucified (Jesus Christ), or they try to escape their destiny, unsuccessfully (Jonah).

They are called Prophets.

The Jewish religion says that Malachi was the last prophet. There must have been some bureaucrat in Jewish history who decided to "close the book" and stop change.

I suggest to you that whenever there is change there are going to be people who have a message to deliver, a new or a refurbished one about how to survive—emotionally and spiritually—the confusion and the pain that change brings about. Moses, who according to the Jewish religious tradition was the greatest prophet of them all, lived during the emanci-

1. Adizes Insights, April 2013.

pation of the Hebrews from slavery. Jesus lived during the Roman times when the Hebrews were experiencing major turmoil. Muhammad, too, lived during a time of change.

Prophets are born all the time and prophesize in times of social change. Major change. There are minor prophets today, each one with a message of his own. The different living Masters who come to us from India are an example.

There are also false messiahs, false prophets: the different gurus, the flavor of the week, the best sellers who make a fortune and disappear into oblivion.

> *For me, Karl Marx as a prophet is dead.*

Jesus was a most dominant and significant prophet, because he channeled a message that was not only appropriate for his times, but, as it turns out, was a message for eternity. It was all about love.

Who can be against that?

And he died. Not for our sins. (I take responsibility for my sins and no one else should die for them.) He died because he deviated from the behavior accepted at the time, which made it look as though he was starting a revolution that threatened those in power.

This story repeats itself throughout history....

Was he the son of God? Not literally. We are all sons of God. He was the chosen son. From the chosen people. Chosen in the sense that he served as a conduit, a channel, for a message from the eternal value system I call God.

Did resurrection occur?

Sure. Anyone with a powerful message lives, especially someone who delivers a message that has validity throughout time. Not literally. Not physically. But in spirit. They live as long as their message is still valid.

For me, Karl Marx as a prophet is dead. His message, also delivered during a time of major social change (the industrialization of Europe), was not valid. It did not survive. (Thank God.)

Jesus Christ lives because his message continues to impact people's lives.

I not only accept Jesus, but I have no difficulty following the words that Jesus Christ brought to people. I support those words, those sentiments.

I do not support the bureaucratic part of the religion. The rituals. The rejection of those who do not follow the rituals.

We all share the same values. That is what counts for me. Not the form. Not the rituals. Not the symbols and stories that people recount and believe occurred. They believe that those stories literally occurred while for me they are metaphors, analogies.

It is the (A) in our mind which prevents us from comprehending the (I) message.

It is the (A) of religion that separates us from each other.

If we focused on the (I), we would find we are all one.

REFLECTIONS ON CHRISTMAS[1]

TOMORROW IS CHRISTMAS EVE. I am going to a church across the street to celebrate.

I am Jewish and I am not converting. So, why am I going?

Jesus was Jewish. Born Jewish. He was circumcised and probably had a bar mitzvah. I am thrilled and excited that tomorrow night millions of people around the world will celebrate, sing hymns, appreciate, and glorify another Jew.

We Jews have been prosecuted, murdered, and burned at the stake for two thousand years, so it pleases me that on at least one evening a year we are appreciated for our contribution to humanity.

And there is a lot to appreciate. Jesus preached and brought a great religion of love and tolerance to the world. Very spiritual.

The fact that over the years his followers became "bureaucratic"—stuck to the dogma and forgot the spirit, forgot love and promoted hate—is not his fault. If he were on earth when this took place Jesus would have denounced them just as he denounced the Jews who were de-sanctifying the temple during his own time.

On that note let me wish you all a Merry Christmas and Happy New Year.

1. Adizes Insights, December 2013.

ON FORGIVING WISHES
FOR THE NEW YEAR[1]

D O YOU REALIZE that it is easy to forgive someone you do not know very well, while it is very difficult to forgive those you are close to? The closer emotionally that person is, the more difficult it is to forgive. That is why family feuds are so painful and prolonged. That is why divorces are an emotional disaster. And fights among siblings are a war.

Psychologists say that we finally mature when we forgive our parents. All of us have some grudge against our parents. Welcome to the club. And we hold on to this grudge for years. We see a therapist, maybe several therapists, for years, trying to forgive. It is not easy. Why? Because we loved them. Or expected to be loved by them. It is much easier to forgive a person you do not love that much. Do not care for much.

Now, who is the person closest to us? Closer than our spouse or child? Closer than a brother, sister, or parent?

Of course, it is ourselves.

It is very difficult to forgive oneself for whatever we feel guilty about. We suffer the most. The longest. And if our refusal to forgive persists it can turn into self-hate. Not a pretty picture.

Interesting that all religions promote the idea of "forgiving," and at the same time preach love. How do we reconcile those opposing prescriptions, since if we love, we will have difficulty forgiving?

But is that always true? Some loving couples do forgive each other. Which means it is doable, to love and forgive—but how?

Apparently the way to reconcile is the sequence by which we love and forgive.

1. Adizes Insights, January 2014.

Here is one sequence: Forgive first. Love second. ("I will love you if I can forgive you.") Difficult. It is conditional love. It would not work.

How about a second sequence: Love first. Now forgive those you love. It works, if it is a true, honest, non-judgmental, non-needy love. Like a loving mother forgives a child for whatever. Love is above all transgressions. She forgives because there is no other way; she loves her child unconditionally.

Start with loving and forgiving yourself. And who is it you are supposed to love first of all as a precondition to forgiving? The insight: love yourself.

Why?

If you love yourself you will have a better chance to forgive yourself and eventually others, too.

But why should I forgive myself or others?

It is because of the value imbedded in forgiving.

When you hold onto guilt or blame yourself or others, you wind up spending a great deal of unnecessary and unhelpful energy. It is not positive energy. It "eats you up." It makes you sick. It is what I call a source of "internal marketing," and in the process it interferes with the positive energy necessary for love to flourish.

The worst "energy sucker" is hate. It will age us prematurely. We become ill, and might even die. Sometimes by our own hand.

So love, and love deeply, honestly, so that you can forgive yourself and others. Do not try to understand. Just do it. Love without questioning anyone or anything. No cost-benefit calculations. No doubting oneself. Just be unconditionally loving.

Start with loving and forgiving yourself. Loving and forgiving others next looks more probable.

The Jewish religion is very practical. Once a year on Yom Kippur we fast and pray, and forgive ourselves and ask forgiveness of others. By the time the day is over we are supposed to start the new year clean and guilt free. And during that day-long fast, repetitively we confirm our love of God.

When we bury our loved ones we tend to be angry with God. We refuse to forgive Him for taking our dear one away forever. But the religion orders us to give a prayer—*yitgadal ve yitkadash shme raba*—where we glorify God and reconfirm our love to God *nevertheless*. Love and forgive.

It is interesting how practical the Jewish religion is. Since the religious sages knew that it is very difficult to love and forgive, the prayer is in Aramaic, so most people who recite it do not understand what they are saying. If they understood they might have difficulty reciting the prayer....

Life tests the depth of our love each time an event happens that requires forgiveness. Life is one long test of love. Those who pass the test with unwavering love, and thus are able to forgive, simply live longer.

So, have your own Yom Kippur and start every New Year by forgiving everyone and everything. And most of all, by forgiving yourself. Let us start every New Year free. Free of guilt and full with love. To live longer.

On that note, may I wish you a long life and a Happy New Year.

Amen.

INSIGHTS FROM PASSOVER NIGHT[1]

WHY DID THE HEBREWS WANDER in the desert for forty years, looking for the Promised Land? Could not God, the all-powerful, the One who knows it all, have shown them the way and gotten them there sooner?

The story of the Exodus can be seen as an allegory, the moral of which is: The road from slavery to freedom is not a straight line. Those with the slave mentality wandered in that desert till they died—and that tells us that it takes a lifetime to traverse the "desert of slavery" in search of the Promised Land, where one is free.

Take me, for instance. I am enslaved to bread. Others are addicted to sugar, to alcohol, to sex, to work, or to their political beliefs.

Come to think of it, who is free? We are all slaves to something that governs our lives. We all spend our lifetimes wandering through the "desert" trying to free ourselves, struggling to find the elusive Promised Land of continuous happiness.

How did the Hebrews become enslaved in Egypt? In the Hebrew language, they did not "go" to Egypt, they "descended" ("*vayered mitzrayma*").

The word "descended" can be understood from a geographic point of view, because Egypt is located south of Canaan, but there is also an allegorical explanation. Jacob went to Egypt because there was no food in Canaan at the time. He took his family to Egypt for a very innocent reason: to survive. But what happened? Over time, his descendants "descended" into slavery by staying too long in a country that was not theirs.

Isn't that how the process of enslavement always happens? We never

1. Adizes Insights, April 2011.

intend to become enslaved to cigarettes, right? We just want some pleasure, so we light one. And then we take another one, and another one, and over time, what happens? We "descend." We become enslaved to smoking. Or to alcohol. Or to work. Many pleasures start innocently but, over time, if repeated, end up enslaving us.

Leadership in the Passover story

Who is Moses, the leader who takes the Hebrews from slavery to freedom? He is a rebel: the adopted son of the Pharaoh, who rebels against those who raised him. He is a murderer. (He kills a fellow Egyptian overseer who is beating a Jewish slave.) And on top of that, his stutter makes him a poor communicator. Is he not the most improbable person to be anointed as the leader?

If a person is not born a leader, then how does he become one?

A true leader follows his conscience.

Here, the story of Passover gives us another insight. Moses was not born a leader. He was instructed by God, who manifested Himself in a bush that burned but was not consumed, to lead his people out of slavery.

The eternally burning bush illustrates that God has no beginning and no end ("*blee reshit*" or "with no beginning"). What else has neither beginning nor end? Our souls. And it is our souls, which reside in our hearts, that connect us to God.

Thus, who is this God that Moses listens to? Whom does a true leader listen to?

A true leader follows his conscience. Follows his heart. Listens to his soul. In that way, he follows God's will.

So should you. We can be all leaders. What makes one a leader is the search for the Promised Land, leading us away from slavery toward freedom. How does the leader accomplish this? By being a follower—by following God's will. By following his or her heart.

The Promised Land is not *there*. It is *here*, in our hearts.

But it's not easy. Moses died across the Jordan River from the Promised Land. He could see it in the distance, but he never did set foot in it.

Why was God so cruel to Moses, who had dedicated his whole life to God and to leading the stubborn, rebellious Hebrews to the Promised Land? The Bible gives the explanation that it was God's punishment for some transgression.

I have a different opinion. I believe this story, too, is an allegory, and its meaning is that no true leader can ever reach the Promised Land. True leaders can only see it from a distance, because for true leaders the Promised Land is a moving target, a horizon that moves as the followers move.

If a leader does reach his goal, it means that he has stopped leading: He has stopped setting new targets, has stopped noticing the movements of the horizon. At some point, he has stopped changing and growing.

Who can lead us from slavery?

All of us who decide to listen to our hearts are leaders, leading ourselves toward freedom. As we listen to our hearts, as we struggle to emancipate ourselves from our dependencies, we learn and we grow. And if we are true leaders, we never stop listening till we die because there is no end to learning, to following God's will.

There is no *point* of enlightenment; there is no specific *location* where the Promised Land can be found. It is not a destination. Enlightenment occurs when you realize that it is the *search* for enlightenment that is enlightening.

Getting free of our enslavements is not as simple as just hopping over to the Promised Land, the land of freedom from enslavement. It takes a lifetime of struggling, of resisting temptations, of worshiping false Gods and then seeking redemption.

The road to heaven is not a straight line. There is no map, no GPS. Granted, established religions try to provide "a manual" (the Bible, for example, or the Quran), but in the Passover Haggadah the wandering slaves in spirit follow God who appears as an elusive cloud, something that cannot be touched or caught. It is not a place or a thing that one can possess; rather it is something that needs to be explored and interpreted to be understood.

Our heart gives us new answers as we listen. The search for the Promised Land is a process. It is a journey, not a destination; the process of continuously learning and growing, continuously listening to our soul, to our conscience.

The Promised Land is not where you are going to, or where you are coming from. It is where you are right now: searching, listening, being conscious.

Each year, as we sit and read the Haggadah and tell the story of the Emergence from Egypt (*Yetziat Mitzrayeem*), the story of how we were freed from our enslavement, we remind ourselves that being freed is not a one-shot deal. It is a lifetime task that never ends.

What Makes Us Human?[1]

IN MY LECTURES, I claim that everything has a life, even stones. There are old stones and new stones. There are young stars and old stars. And, of course, there are new and old cars. All have a lifecycle.

What is the difference between, say, a stone and a tree or an animal? And what is the difference between us humans and animals?

Here is my insight:

The difference between inanimate objects and animate objects is, among other things, that inanimate objects do not reproduce themselves. When a stone breaks to pieces for whatever reason, or a star explodes, it is not reproducing itself; it is just falling apart.

Now, what distinguishes trees and vegetables from animals of any kind? It is the brain: the capability of processing information using the brain, which is called reasoning.

And what distinguishes us humans from animals? We have lungs and hearts and reproductive organs, as they do; and brains, as they do. Admittedly, the human brain is bigger—but is that the major difference, the size of our brains? Then what about disabled children who are born with brains that are deficient by human standards? Should we describe them as animals? I would say no.

So what is the difference?

Have you ever seen an animal build a temple in order to worship something? Obviously not.

Humans have a system of beliefs.

1. Adizes Insights, April 2011.

What about the Nazis? They had a system of beliefs, too, didn't they? Their belief was that they were called to dominate the world. Were they human, then? They had all the ingredients of being human that animals do not have—symbols, the ability to write and read—but they were not all human. Some of the Nazis had no heart. Otherwise, there is no explanation for how they could have taken innocent children to the ovens.

Animals have no God, but not all "gods" are equal. There are false gods—idols. Mammon is one of them. The Nazi swastika, which symbolized the superiority of one race over all others, was another idol.

But is that the major difference, the size of our brains?

The true God is the God of love, the one we serve with our *hearts*.

Those who worship idols, false gods and do not listen to the heart are animals disguised in a human body.

The more we listen to our hearts, the more human we are. We have more than consciousness; we have a conscience.

Animals focus on survival. We as humans feel for what is around us, not only for other human beings but also for the suffering of animals and the health of trees, rivers and mountains and the air and oceans. We care because, in addition to the necessary tools for finding a reproductive mate (long-term survival) and for finding food and shelter (immediate survival), our thoughts and feelings transcend the necessary. Our hearts ache and our consciences bother us, because we humans have a sense of right and wrong. We go *beyond* survival. We listen to the heart which, may I suggest, animals do not.

Reflections from My Stay in an Ashram[1]

I HAVE COME TO CHENNAI, INDIA, to the Babuji Ashram, an Ashram of the Sahaj Marg mission, to meditate and meet Master Chariji again.

This, I believe, is my third or fourth trip to India for that purpose in seven years. I wish I would have come annually. Each time I learn something that, in retrospect, changes my life for the better. Deeply. Significantly.

I have reported my insights from meditation in past blogs. What did I learn this time, on the first day of my arrival?

Master Chariji is eighty-seven years old. He is also seriously sick. His days are counted. Or maybe it is months, but it does not look like he has years left. So, I wondered, what does a person who knows that his days are counted, who faces the inevitable, what does he think is really important in life?

Usually a person in that situation, I thought, kind of evaluates his life and has insights into what he could have done differently and better. He will refocus on what really counts in life so that those days that are left to live are not wasted anymore.

Sitting next to Master Chariji, a privilege I cherish and value tremendously, I asked him: "Master, what is really important to you, *now*?"

As I say, I expected some deep insight about life, a kernel of knowledge that I assumed a person facing death would have.

His answer: "Nothing new. The same."

Now, stop and reflect on his answer to my question "What is important to you now?" The answer: "Nothing new. The same."

1. Adizes Insights, May 2014.

Can you see how integrated this person is? He has no remorse about anything he did in his life and there is no need to change anything in the time left in his life. Truly living in the present. Past and future are all in the present. Or, said differently, the past continues through the present into the future. There is no difference. He is totally at peace with himself. Nothing needs to change. There was no waste in the past that he needs to catch up in the present before the future evaporates. What is, is. What was meant to be, is meant to be. Free. Free from remorse. Free from guilt. Free from wishful thinking. Free. Free to live. Free to die peacefully.

What a way to live! What a way to die!

I asked him, although he looked so old and feeble and I know he was in serious pain, if I would be able to see him privately.

"If I can be of service to you, yes," he said.

Wait a moment…the guy is dying, and he is going to give the scarce minutes left to serve me or anyone else!

Is that what life is about, then?

Past and future are all in the present. Stop and think. Stop and reflect: What else is life about? Is it a waste to be of utility to others? In those remaining days of ones life, most people, I think, would rather serve themselves. Old people become kind of selfish. They cherish every second of life left to be used by and for themselves. Why waste time on others?

Why was his answer different? In Sahaj Marg meditation you open your heart and that means you love. And to love is to give of yourself to others.

LIFE IS LOVE. Without love what is life all about? And love without giving is all talk and no being.

To love you have to stop expecting. What is meant to be will be. No less. No more. This meditation teaches you to stop expecting and to take life as is. Do not fight life. Live life. Loving.

Now the question is what is life? What does it mean to live?

How do you know you are alive? Is it that you can move your hands and legs? Or that you can breathe? But there are people who are paralyzed who are alive, and you can stop breathing for a minute and you are still alive Ah, then was Descartes right: "I *think* therefore I am?" I am not so sure. Some people do not think and they are alive. So what is the answer?

I said: "Since I feel, I am alive." When I stop feeling whatever I feel, when I am just a body without a soul, there is no life for me.

But what does it mean to feel? How do you know that you feel? (Thank you Deepak.)

In order to feel, you have to be conscious. And in order to be conscious you need to be present. Here and now. Not to let your mind wonder all the time into the past or into the future. Meditation helps you to be here and now. To be present. To be conscious and thus to feel. And thus to be alive.

Whoa. Think about it.

Working hard. Rushing from one assignment to another. In my case, jumping from one airplane to another, from one client to another, scared to waste time—time is money, no?—I am not present. I am not conscious. It looks like I am alive, running like a mad man, for only God knows what it is I am chasing… and the harder I fill my time with activities so I do not waste any time, the faster time flies, and I have no idea where years of my life have gone. No time to feel. No time to be. Thus, no time to live. To be alive.

But if meditation is so good, why don't I do it every day? Why?

Because to sit and do nothing and let thoughts come freely to your head and not try to control them and manipulate them is *hard*.

Yes, it is hard *being*. And very easy to be busy *doing*.

To really live is scary. To fill your life with action so it looks like you are alive is easy.

When Do We Die?[1]

IMAGINE A PERSON SITTING IN A ROOM full of people debating a subject. This person does not say a word. Does not express himself even through body language.

You would say that this person is not really there. He is physically there but that is all.

Now imagine the same room with the same people debating a subject and repetitively quoting someone. Is that "someone" in the room? Not physically, but otherwise he is fully engaged and "alive."

May I suggest there are two ways to exist: physically and interactively.

Some people pass through life unnoticed. They have been here physically, but when they perish physically, they perish totally.

We die twice: once physically and the second time when no one remembers us.

Is Buddha alive? Not physically but interactively very much so. Is Jesus Christ alive? For sure. Moses and even Hitler, with the rise of the neo-Nazis around the word.

How about Karl Marx? I would say he is either dead or dying.

To remain alive one has to do something memorable while physically alive. What is that something?

There is a difference between Hitler and Buddha or Jesus Christ.

One had a destructive impact. The other a constructive impact. Destructive means he preached and is still preaching destruction and hate through his work and followers. The other preached growth and love.

1. Adizes Insights, May 2014.

Neither can be forgotten but one is preferable to the other. And, may I also suggest that those who are presently and interactively offering love "live" longer.

However, there is more to this notion that we do not actually die. Physically yes, but interactively no.

We carry in our genes the style and physical characteristics of our ancestors. And, I suggest, we also carry their fears and hopes. Which means they live through us; they are still "alive."

There is a difference, however, between physical life and interactive life.

In physical life, we experience joy directly. Joy from the pleasure of food, intimacy, socialization, and intellectual stimulation. None of which we experience when we are only interactively present.

Or maybe, we just postulate that we are not enjoying it anymore. Because none of us knows for sure what life thereafter offers.

Part IV

✳

Tools for Life

All Problems Are Just a Test[1]

L ET ME SUGGEST that we all have the same goal: At the end of the day we are all looking for unconditional, total, absolute integration. Enlightenment. Total peace. Heaven. Nirvana. *Samadhi*. Getting closer to God. All these expressions have the same connotation for me: *total integration*—which means no problems, nothing to worry about. No energy wasted. Peace.

Nearly everything we do is part of our attempt to reach that state of being.

Now, if we define total integration as a goal, there is a problem: It is impossible to reach this goal, because of change.

Change causes disintegration. Change causes disintegration. How? Everything in this world is a system and systems are composed of subsystems, which, when there is change, do not change in synchronicity. In personal life, for example: We could be physically forty years old, because we were born forty years ago, but with great learning experiences, we may be intellectually in our seventies, while emotionally still teenagers and spiritually not even born yet.

Change causes the disintegration of the system, and disintegration is manifested in what we call problems—our name for the various cracks and breakdowns in the system.

Notice that when a person has a lot of problems, his friends will say the guy is "falling apart," he is "coming unglued." The same could be said of a company that is experiencing rapid change that they cannot handle.

1. Adizes Insights, December 2011.

Since the cause of all problems is disintegration, the solution to all problems is integration. Integration is a function of mutual trust and respect: the more MT&R, the more integration.

I have begun to see every problem as a test, a challenge: Do I have within me the self trust and respect to deal with my problem, and the mutual trust and respect with others with whom I share the problem? I am being tested. The bigger the test I can handle, the stronger I become.

Life is one long series of tests.

LIFE IS A GAME OF CARDS[1]

I RECENTLY HEARD THE EXPRESSION "You have to play the cards you're dealt," and it reminded me how similar life really is to a game of cards—in multiple ways.

First, you can't control how many cards there are, or which ones you get. Any attempt to control it (like hiding a card up your sleeve) is cheating. You have to play the cards given to you. Sometimes you get good cards. Sometimes they are lousy.

Just like in life, evaluating each card alone will not give you an accurate view of what you have. The cards are interdependent: The value of each card is determined by its importance to the whole hand.

And isn't that like life? Every new situation has its threats and its opportunities. There are strengths and there are weaknesses. See the totality. Do not overlook the forest by focusing on a single tree.

Now, what happens when you get lousy cards? You fold and wait for the next round, right? That is how life should be taken: Fold and wait for the next round. There's no use complaining to the dealer (in the case of life, that would be God Almighty). It's not productive to get depressed or angry about the cards you've been dealt. They are what they are. If necessary, fold and look forward to the next round. As another expression goes "Whenever one door closes, another opens."

Here is another moral we can learn from cards: If you get bad cards in one round and decide to fold, make sure you don't also fold your spirit. If you make the mistake of getting all worked up, you might be given a good set of cards in the next round, yet be so distracted by the last round that you miss an opportunity to win.

1. Adizes Insights, April 2013.

Remember: Each round is brand new.

Come to think of it, how many people have difficulty developing a bond with someone new because they were hurt in a previous relationship? How many people have difficulty starting a new job because the last one was a disaster?

Life presents you with a series of "hands." Just play the ones you're dealt, and remember that each round is a new round, with brand-new opportunities to win, as well as new opportunities to fail. Enjoy the game. Enjoy life, in spite of its ups and downs—or, perhaps, because of them.

Once you identify the players, learn their style.

Another lesson: Always make sure to look around and ask yourself, "What game are we playing? What is at stake here? What are the rules of this game? What does it mean to win?"

Think about the many military people who retire and go to work for a civilian corporation neglecting to make a crucial switch in their heads, to realize that now they are playing a different game. Or businessmen who go into politics. It is not the same game. The rules are different, and so are the criteria for winning.

Furthermore, you must always know who the players are and how many of them are playing. You cannot play solo, in cards or in life, so it is crucial to identify the players and the stakeholders.

How many times have we lost a round because we were dealing with one person at the table, only to find out later that the one who was actually calling the shots was someone else—someone who was not even at the table.

One last analogy: Once you identify the players, learn their style. Find out what drives them. Observe their strategy; often that will tell you what cards they have and what they are looking for. After all, they, too, must play the cards they were dealt.

Some people do not like to play cards. That's okay. You can skip playing card games, but you cannot skip playing the cards of life.

Life Is Conflict, Frustration, and Pain. Necessarily So?[1]

IDO NOT KNOW IF IT IS TRUE FOR YOU, but I often find myself in considerable pain because of conflicts or because life does not yield what I want.

One day while lecturing about management I suddenly realized I was not, in fact, lecturing about management and corporations; I was also lecturing about myself. I was talking about my life.

It was borne home to me that life is painful, and filled with conflicts. And all of that is inevitable.

Here is the insight: We all know there is change. Change has been here forever and, I hope, will continue to be here forever. Change is life. Only death halts change.

Change, by definition, means that something new has happened. There is a new event that impacts us. Now we need to decide what to do. It is like coming to an intersection we encounter for the first time and are forced to choose: left, right, straight ahead, back, or stay in place.

Making decisions in the face of a new fact or situation necessarily means deciding under the stress of uncertainty: Not all the relevant information is available. The whole picture only becomes clear after the fact.

The result is that when we try to deal with uncertainty we are confronted with conflicts: what to do, how to do it, when to do it, and, of course, who should do it. Each of these variables requires individual attention, even though they are interdependent.

A decision is not real until implemented, and to implement a decision we must be willing to take risks.

1. Adizes Insights, March 2013.

How do we handle risk? By debating it in our head, which acts like a mini-parliament: Liberal thoughts tell us to go ahead and take the risk while conservative thoughts tell us to beware and slow down.

All in all, we do not sleep well at night as we face life's turbulence.

If making the decision requires contributions from other people, and the implementation requires the cooperation of other stakeholders, the conflict, the frustrations, and the pain are all magnified.

How do we find comfort in life and avoid the pain life pushes on us?

Easy. Go to an ashram or find a cave and meditate all day long all your life. Stop change. Disassociate from life. Disassociate from doing. Stop contributing to this world.

But that is not a life most of us know or choose to live. Nor one I wish to live.

In short, accept life. Embrace it. What other choice do we have? Accept life's pain and the conflicts that accompany it. In short, accept life. Embrace it. And stop dreaming about some Garden of Eden where there is no pain. The moment we ate from that tree of knowledge we chose pain and conflict in an effort to know and understand the life around us. That is part of the package of choosing knowledge.

The expression "Life is a bitch and then you die" is not just a joke or a funny statement. It is a fact of life one has to accept.

Can the pain be made more bearable? Can the conflict be constructive?

Yes, and the answer is present in MT&R.

If there is mutual trust and respect, conflict between people is not just bearable, but it enhances growth. And if there is self trust and self respect, the conflict inside ourselves becomes an opportunity for learning and growing.

My Jazz Revelation[1]

I REALLY HATED MODERN JAZZ. There is no melody—or at least that is what I thought—just a diarrhea of sound that gave me a headache.

Well, as God would want it, my 17-year-old son is a fanatical aficionado of jazz. He plays the saxophone and studies jazz at a boarding school that specializes in music. Every summer he attends jazz summer camps. He practices his scales till his lips are swollen. He sleeps with jazz music playing on his computer all night long.

I, on the other hand, love folk music, which he absolutely hates. Once, when I was listening to Bulgarian women singing in harmony, he remarked that their singing sounded as if they were having "a real bad time with their period."

As you can see, we were not really "sharing."

But this summer, he asked me to join his summer jazz workshop at the University of Louisville, Kentucky. He wanted me to bring my accordion and learn to play jazz, so we could have something in common.

I took him on. With trepidation. Not only did I hate jazz, I also do not know how to read music. I play by ear and only in the C-major scale.

How was I going to fit in?

Upon arriving, I discovered that there were 400 bass, guitar, drum, piano, sax, and trombone players, but only one pitiful polka accordion player: me.

This is going to be humiliating, I thought.

But, on the other hand, what an opportunity to be vulnerable, to get out of my safety zone and see what would happen.

1. Adizes Insights, July 2011.

Go and surprise yourself, I said to myself. And a surprise it was, proving that getting out of your safety zone can be a rewarding growth experience despite the pain.

The workshop was five days long, starting every day at 8 a.m. and ending after midnight with a concert and jam sessions.

Learning something totally new means being subjected to change, and change is like burying your past. So it should not come as a surprise that as part of the experience, you traverse the five stages of grief that Elisabeth Kübler-Ross wrote about.

First was Denial: Why am I here? I do not even like jazz. Then I moved to the Anger phase, becoming furious at my son for bringing me into a situation where I would certainly be humiliated by my ignorance.

On the second day, after Denial and Anger, I entered the Bargaining phase: If I just sit in a class and listen, maybe I will learn something.

Depression was next: I was assigned to a band. All the members were playing their instruments, while I just sat there like a mouse in the rain, hugging my accordion like a child clutching his teddy bear. I could not play anything. I was miserable.

I finally started enjoying the week after I entered the Acceptance stage: Okay, so I *am* ignorant; so what?

Focus on your goal, I told myself. You did not come here to learn to play. You came to learn what jazz is all about and to bond with your son.

How easy it is to forget our goals and get sidetracked by experiences that overwhelm us.

And what did I learn? I learned that jazz is a whole separate language of music.

Playing jazz in a combo is a musical conversation.

If you listen to people conversing in a language you do not know—say, Wolof, which is spoken in Senegal—it will sound meaningless to you, like random sounds. But once you learn the language, then you start understanding the conversation.

Playing jazz in a combo is a musical conversation. Like any language, it has rules and a structure. Jazz even has "dialects." The rules for playing bebop are different from the rules for swing, cool jazz, or free jazz. It is the same language—a bebop musician will understand what a cool jazz musician is playing—but each has a unique musical construct.

You really know a language when you can tell a joke in that language, and jazz has its own sense of humor. Sometimes in their "conversations," the solo instruments tease each other musically, and by the time they finish playing everyone is laughing.

Contrary to what I always believed, there is a melody in jazz. It is played first, then each player in his or her turn improvises on the chords of that melody. That is the structure—the sequence of the chords following the melody—but there are countless improvisations each player can make within each chord. Thus, although they are playing the same piece, they usually do not repeat the same music. Using language as an analogy, we would say that if several people tell the same story, each would tell it differently.

Thus, jazz is a structured form of creativity. Each player is, in a sense, a composer, but since the musicians all play together there must be a structure that unites their playing.

This reminded me of the Adizes Methodology for team problem solving: Each participant has and follows his own distinct style, free to make his unique contribution, while Adizes provides the structure to lead the discussion so that the team can work together.

At one of the performances that week, a very famous musician gave what I thought was a terrible performance: high, shrill sounds on the sax that sounded more like screams than like music.

Who taught him to play? I wondered, and how can he be famous when he can't even get normal sounds out of his instrument?

The next day at breakfast, I mentioned to another sax player that I thought the previous night's performance had been embarrassing. I had seriously thought of leaving during the intermission.

He looked at me as if he was a Muslim and I had just told him I'd burned the Quran.

"What are you talking about? I had tears in my eyes!" he exclaimed. "It was an unbelievable experience. It was a privilege to listen to him."

Now I felt like a person who discovers his pants are torn and his rear end is showing…without underwear.

The musician the previous night had been playing "free jazz," which has no rules. The instrument is manipulated to express the musician's feelings. Honestly. Openly. Truly. Freely. All his pain, despair, anger, and hope. The man was falling apart emotionally and telling it to us through the sounds he was creating.

Oh my God, I said to myself. I realized I needed to (and I did) apologize to my son. His music was his way of communicating his feelings to me; when I criticized his music, in a sense I was criticizing, possibly even negating, his feelings.

What did I learn from this?

To have a smaller mouth and bigger ears. To talk less and hear more. Not to judge at all—period. There is a reason for everything that happens. Just watch and experience. Think less. Feel more.

And that is exactly how good jazz musicians play.

When they practice, they will play scales, chords, up and down and back and forth, for hours. But when they are improvising, they do not think about what to play. They simply allow the music to take its own path.

When jazz musicians improvise, perhaps they are themselves acting as instruments, to allow something bigger (God?) to come through.

This reminds me of meditation: The goal is to calm your mind and let your *heart* speak—your heart, where God dwells.

Bio-energetic healing, which I recently studied, is similar: You are not the healer. You make yourself a conduit for cosmic energy, which passes through you to heal your patient. And the same for Reiki.

Come to think of it, the same is true for everything we do creatively. I have this experience when I write. Like right now: I am not thinking about what to say. It just flows out of me, if I let it, by not thinking and not judging. Thinking blocks the energy. Our egos interfere with the creative process.

It helps to see ourselves as instruments of something larger. We are like the saxophone, which does not perform but is the instrument with which the player communicates.

Ah, thinking like this makes you humble. It is not you who is great. (Golda Meir once remarked to someone: "Don't be so humble. You are not that great.") You can become greater by being humble and understanding that it is God that does it all—God as endless cosmic energy with consciousness of right and wrong.

We are great when we realize how small we are.

On Diversity[1]

IAM IN MOSCOW walking on the treadmill, watching a video screen. I am watching CNN. They are airing a program on diversity.

It occurred to me that diversity is approached from a political and ethical angle. That it is politically correct to promote diversity, that we are all equal, have the same rights, etc., and ethical in that it is immoral to discriminate.

I believe a very important point is being missed: Diversity is good for you. We should pursue diversity because it is a win-win proposition. It serves our self-interests.

How?

Start with the assumption that no one is perfect. Thus we need others to complement us. But to complement us, those "others" have to be different. Thus diversity is necessary for growth, for learning, for synergy.

Years ago I was listening to a blind person delivering a motivational speech. Something he said impressed me: "I am blind from birth. I have a deficiency. But how about you? Do you have any limitation? How about some emotional limitation, or intellectual limitation?"

In other words, we are all "blind" in something. The question is what are we doing about our limitations?

This speaker was telling us how he became a motivational speaker, how he learned to play music in spite of being blind. How about you, me, anyone else? Are you overcoming your weaknesses?

Who is the hero? Who can overcome his own liabilities?

I have a first cousin who has the same name I do, except he spells it

1. Adizes Insights, April 2012.

differently in English: Yitzhak Adijes. He was also born blind. But he won the world championship for blind sailing. He overcame his limits.

Does this inspire you? Does that motivate you to overcome your limits, too?

It sure inspired me.

We can be chronologically seventy-five but feel and act as if we are forty-five.

We learn from diversity because those "other" people have, by definition, what we don't have. The Africans, for example, have a soul in their laughter, in their music, in their dancing, that we white westerners have much less.

Again, diversity enriches.

I find gypsies inspiring too. They live the moment. They know how to enjoy life to its fullest. There is much to learn from them.

For me, this learning does not stop just with people who are physically handicapped, or with those whose color, religion, or sex is different. One can learn from horses, from dogs, and from stones.

I remember how, in studying a stone, I realized the difference between chronological age and conscious age. We humans are the only ones who, by being conscious, can impact our emotional age. Stones, trees, and animals have no control over their age. We can be chronologically seventy-five but feel and act as if we are forty-five. We can control our age by what we eat, how stressful our life is, what we do (love what you do and you will not age as fast, for instance), etc.

We can learn from everything. The Old Testament says, "Go to the ant and learn from its ways."

Diversity is the source of learning. Sameness is barren.

Embrace diversity, not only because it is politically and ethically correct, but because there is so much for you to learn and benefit from.

THE EUROPEAN CUP
SOCCER GAMES[1]

I AM WATCHING THE GAMES, and I have noticed the advertising. The first ad says, "Celebrate Diversity." The ad that follows says, "Respect."

Wait a minute. I do not know if my lifetime work has anything to do with it, or if they came to the same conclusions independently, but notice what it says: *Celebrate Diversity*. I have been writing in my books and on my blog for years now that we should not simply *tolerate* diversity, we should *celebrate* it, because we benefit from it.

There are many programs on tolerance; there are museums of tolerance, school programs on tolerance. However, this is misguided thinking, because tolerance is to suffer quietly. Tolerance implies surrendering. It does not give you energy like celebrating does.

To *celebrate* is different. Celebration means to welcome something, not merely let it be.

Why celebrate?

Because there is no progress without diversity. There is no innovation without welcoming and encouraging diversity. Compare the desert, where there is no diversity, to the jungle.

And it is also constructive if there is Mutual Respect which is the second slogan of the Cup.

I am moved. I do not care whether I had something to do with the European Cup. I *do* care that someone at the European Cup is thinking right.

1. Adizes Insights, July 2012.

THE MEANING OF MONEY[1]

WHAT IS "MONEY?" For some people, "money" is a means of survival. It enables them to place food on the table, provide shelter, and pay for medical expenses when the need arises. Often these are the people who earn very little and struggle to make ends meet.

However, what about those who have much more than what is needed for food, shelter, and medical care? Here money plays a different role. For some, it becomes a measurement of self-worth: "Can you believe how much they are willing to pay for my services?" For others, money serves as a form of displayed wealth, a way to gain respect and status in the eyes of others.

Money can also function to allocate scarce resources, like time. You raise your fees so that only those who can pay receive the desired service. Money serves as a screening vehicle. This is done with any scarce resource—not only time, but jewelry, diamonds, gold, etc. Money can also be used to secure people's cooperation. You can use money to solve a problem, which without money would be difficult to attempt.

The above are the usual explanations of money's value. I came across two meanings given to money that I was not aware of before that I want to share with you.

Ladd, a friend of mine who is quite wealthy—though you would not know it because he does not display it—gives the following meaning to money.

"It gives me the freedom to choose," he says.

The more money you have the "free-er" you can be to choose what you

1. Adizes Insights, April 2014.

want to do, when you want to do it, and with whom you want to do it. More money means having more choices.

There is a catch in this interpretation, though. The more choices you want to have, the more money you need. However, to have more money means you must work more hours and expend more time and effort to earn it. It can consume you, which of course can cut down on your choices; time is no longer at your disposal and with less time, your choices narrow considerably.

If you do not spend it, they will.

This meaning of money has validity then, to my way of thinking, for those men and women who have the strength of character to say: "Enough. I have enough money to make freely the choices I desire. Thus, no more money is needed. Enough."

It sounds good, but it is not easy to do because money has an addictive character. To those addicted, the more they have the more they want to have, therefore, they are enslaved to money.

A very rich client (one of the 500 richest men in the world) told me his interpretation of the meaning of money, one that I find particularly appealing. He explained that for him the value of money is determined by how much he enjoyed something; thus, this determined how much he spent.

Think about it. Money's value is related to how much pleasure you derive from it. Therefore, to enjoy it, you have to spend it.

Take someone who made millions, but in his heart feels poor. He has great difficulty spending his money. Therefore, he lives very, very modestly at a standard of living commensurate with a person who has one hundredth of his net worth. How much money does he have? Only as much as he enjoys it. For that, he has to spend it.

Money in the bank has no meaning unless you derive pleasure simply from counting it and getting a sense of satisfaction and self-worth by the magnitude of your assets.

Tell me how much you are enjoying your money, and I will tell you how much you really have. Money not used is like money not had. It is just a number. When you die, it will go to the government and to your children who will enjoy it. So who is really the rich one here? Who really has the money? Those who enjoy it.

Once, in a private airport, I met someone who had an enormous hangar for his planes. He had a large executive plane and a small one as well; and then there was his small helicopter and a grand one... I asked him why he needed so many flying machines. He looked me in the eye and said, "If you do not spend it, they will".

Is the only answer then to spend the money for self-enjoyment? Or, maybe you can spend it in a way that you will enjoy it doubly?

Yes, there is a way to enjoy money that can be highly gratifying. I refer to philanthropy. It gives you an opportunity to change people's lives for the better. And to make a difference. Now not only you are enjoying your wealth but others are too. Money has now a multiplying effect.

You are only as rich as how much you give to others who need it more.

My conclusion: Money should be a measurement of self-worth, it should give you the choice and freedom to do what your heart wishes. But how wealthy you really are is a function of how much you enjoy using your money, and the most gratifying use is to meet other peoples' needs, too.

THE WALL: AN ALLEGORY[1]

IREMEMBER THE DAY MY LITTLE SON, who at the time was around four years old, was standing next to a wall shouting, "Move!"

Four or forty-four, we often find ourselves up against a problem that we cannot control, but nevertheless try to solve. We try to move "the wall" (a spouse, a boss, a subordinate…you name it). It is analogous to banging your head against the wall. It does not move and all you get for your effort is a headache. What usually follows is the "victim scenario," where we blame the wall for hurting us.

Obviously, it is not the wall's fault. It is our futile attempt to move an immovable object.

All of us who engage in this practice (and I include myself) tend to have a strong ego. We believe we should be able to solve the problem. That we should have control of the situation. To stop banging our head is to admit that we are not omnipotent. Our ego will not accept it.

In a roundabout way, I believe this touches on maturity. To me maturity means recognizing that something that bothers you, because it is neither acceptable nor desirable, is "a wall," and it is necessary to come to terms with it. In other words, you need to recognize and accept your limitations and your limited capabilities.

That is the beginning of maturity.

There is obviously a benefit to being immature. If we were all mature, there would be no change, no revolutions, no breakthroughs; those who make the breakthroughs do not know that it cannot be done.

David Ben-Gurion, the first Prime Minister of Israel, when asked how

1. Adizes Insights, June 2013.

he intended to start a Jewish state surrounded by one hundred million Arabs, said: "Those who do not believe in miracles are not realists."

So, here's my curve ball: I believe that founders of companies, innovators, even charismatic leaders, are immature. They do not accept their limitations. At times, when they succeed, they enrich us with their innovations and their leadership. But, they pay the price in the quality of their personal lives. They often live with a constant headache from banging their head trying to move their "wall."

What should we do then when confronted with the challenge that will not budge? With a wall?

First, we can always continue banging the wall with our head while leveling accusations against it. That is, as I said, futile, immature behavior. But presumably it serves us somehow. It fulfills a need. And we apparently are rewarded with the attention we crave.

Of course, there is another solution: Go around the wall.

And then there is the solution where you surrender.

If the immovable object is a marriage, people find a way to enjoy life outside their miserable marriage. In business, they do the minimum they can for the company and try to maximize their free time, maybe moonlighting somewhere else.

And then there is the solution where you surrender. You simply accept the wall learn to live with it and stop banging your head against it. In business, it is called "the moose." A dead moose is lying in the middle of the room. Everyone knows the moose is there, but no one talks about it. They just live with it.

Why would they do that?

I have seen that happen in companies where the CEO is arrogant, abusive, demeaning. And people still do not leave. They do not even complain. They just live with the situation. Why? Because they get paid far above the market rate; for them the alternative of leaving is too expensive.

Leaving the room for another place, which has no wall to contend with, is the last of the choices we have.

What strategy do you choose if it is not "a wall" that confronts you, but a partition? It looks easy. All you have to do is push it aside.

Not so. The analogy does not serve us well here. A human "partition" does not change because you want him to change. A person—quite different from a partition—has a will of his own. He will change for his own internal reasons, following his own self-interest.

Accusing him of causing your headache—and insisting that because of that he must change—is a waste of time. He will change when it is in his interest to change.

So if you want to cause change you have to ask yourself why it is good for "the partition," the other party, to change not why it is only good for you.

If such self-interest is either not strong enough, or the other party is incapable of moving, it is better to realize you are confronting not a partition but a wall. Now you have the following choices: live with it, walk around it, or walk out of it. But stop banging your head.

Or…

There is one more alternative many people miss. It is to enjoy the wall. Look for the positives. Instead of cursing the rose for having thorns, bless the thorns for having a rose.

Instead of perceiving the wall as blocking our way, can it be perceived as protecting us, blocking external threats?

Is there anything positive in having this wall?

There are no positives without negatives and, by the same token, there are no negatives that have no positives. Can you see them both?

THERE ARE NO MISTAKES[1]

I F AT THE TIME YOU MADE A DECISION you knew it was a mistake, would you have made that decision? Think about it.

It is not logical. Right? We do not consciously make mistakes. Unless we are addicted, say, to something like smoking. Then we light up knowing that it is harmful to our health.

But if we are not addicted, if we are logical and in control of our emotions and our needs, we will make the best decision possible at the time. Like getting married. Or buying a house. Or accepting a job offer.

A mistake is something we beat ourselves up over. Usually the self-recrimination begins *after some time* has passed, after we get more information, develop new insight, and become aware of the undesirable repercussions of our decision.

So "a mistake" is our judgment about a decision we made in the past and now, based on new information, about which we were unaware earlier, regrets have set in.

Obviously it does not make sense.

At the time we decided and took action, we made the best decision we could have at the time. We acted with all the emotional, intellectual, and spiritual capabilities we had at hand.

So what do we gain by beating ourselves over the head for being who we were?

Instead of saying "I made a mistake," we should ask ourselves what there is to learn now that we have new information and new experience. What should we have known, considered, judged, or evaluated differently?

1. Adizes Insights, August 2013.

I would write down the answers to these questions. And periodically read what I have written.

Why? Because we forget the lessons of life and repeat the "mistakes." We all know people who divorced, only to marry a new spouse very similar to their former wife or husband. It becomes a repeating pattern, over and over again.

By writing them down, we articulate the lessons. And by re-reading those notes and observations we are better able to absorb and learn from them.

The notebook with the lessons described and spelled out serves as a reminder not to repeat a decision that we will regret later on and beat ourselves over the head for.

There are no mistakes in life. Only lessons to learn.

To Love What I Hate[1]

I AM ON A VEGAN SOS DIET. (I am on this diet for medical reasons.) This is more than just vegetarian. Vegetarians eat dairy products and eggs. Not vegans. SOS Vegans are even more stringent. They do not eat salt, oil, or sugar.

How do you survive on no meat, no fowl, no fish, no eggs, no cheese, no salt, no oil, no sugar? You cook and eat at home. Forget going out. Forget restaurants. There is no dish there that has no oil or salt. I have tried to find one in fifty-two countries.

While at home, I can follow the diet religiously, but now I am traveling and that means eating out in restaurants. Ordering ahead of time is not a solution, because I do not go to eat alone and who knows where my party will take me. It is tough.

What do I do? I have to cook in my hotel and eat in my room, that's all.

That's all?! Easier said than done, especially since I hate to cook. The most I know how to do is heat water. I have never cooked in my life.

Here I am in Moscow in a suite in a four- or five-star hotel (quite expensive). I bought myself a multi-cooker, some vegetables, spinach spaghetti, quinoa, brown rice, and I got ready to cook.

It was a disaster.

My wife told me to just put the spaghetti in the cooker, put in some water, push the button, and go to work. "When you come back it will be ready," she said. But, she did not tell me *how much* water to put in…. I followed the instructions on the package.

Oh, my God! When I came back from work the machine was overflowing

1. Adizes Insights, November 2012.

with gooey spaghetti all over the carpet. Good thing the machine did not explode. It took me an hour to clean the place so I wouldn't get kicked out of the hotel.

Why did I not let the hotel cook for me? Because I am cheap. The prices in a Moscow hotel are outrageous. A cup of tea in the lobby is $20. I would have to take out a loan from the bank to pay for their custom cooking.

I should give up cooking. Right? Not for me. Right?

Wrong.

What you hate might be what you love.

I fell in love with cooking. This thing I had hated all my life I discovered is quite pleasurable. To experiment. To taste and try again, and to learn how to use this multi-cooker.

It is really a pleasure to eat what you have cooked and not what someone else cooked for you. It is a wonderful new feeling of being in control and being self-sufficient. Being independent. And creative.

What is the insight?

What you hate might be what you love and you do not know until you try it.

What we hate might be what we perceive something to be, and not what it really is. It is all in our head. We confuse perception with reality, as if what we perceive is the reality.

What anything *really* is can be found only by experiencing it.

Hate and love are in our head. But this is not as it should be. We should let experience drive what we love and hate, and through experience, make the choice.

We should let the *is* run the show, not the *should* nor the *want*. Or, said differently, we should let the *is* drive the *want*, and together they should drive the *should*.

Now I am asking myself what else I hate. Let me do it, and do it enough times until I really can say whether or not I hate it. Like exercising. In the past I have followed Bob Hutchins' dictum religiously: "Every time I feel like exercising, I lie down until the feeling passes."

No more. It's time to see if I really hate it.

Too Lazy to Think[1]

THE HIGHER THE RATE OF CHANGE, the higher the instabilities and disruptions in our life.

Change impacts multiple subsystems. On the micro level, the personal level (emotional, intellectual, spiritual, and physical subsystems), on the mezzo level of organizations like corporations (marketing operational financial and human resources systems), and the macro level (economic, social and political institutions). As those system components do not change at the same speed, the situation is becoming increasingly complex.

That means that making decisions is becoming more stressful, more difficult to process.

The result is that people have difficulty thinking clearly and increasingly look for instructions for what to do. They seek formulas, so they do not have to think: Just tell me yes or no.

This search for simple answers to complex problems explains, in part, the fantastic growth in the consulting services industry and the proliferation of coaches and life guides.

When, in my work, I refuse to give an answer to my clients and suggest they use common sense instead, I find them perplexed and somewhat unfulfilled. They want an answer. I suggest instead that they *think*.

Apparently, I am asking too much. In the complex world we live in, finding common sense is not easy. It might even be very difficult to find.

Why? What is entailed in finding common sense?

---

1. Adizes Insights, September 2013.

Common means that it makes sense to all the stakeholders. Finding common sense means civilized exchange of information, and more importantly, exchange of judgment. It means learning from people who do not necessarily agree with you.

This is not easy.

People have less and less time to exchange positions. And less and less patience to hear and listen to each other. Thus they are less and less tolerant and less understanding of each other.

What is the alternative?

I believe the accelerated rate of change with the collateral stressful impact it has on the thinking processes is fueling extremist religious revival in all religions. (And the extremist sections of religions are growing in their extremism.)

The common denominator in both cases is that there is no need to think.

Why is that? Because religion provides a "manual" for what to do and not to do, whether it is Sharia or the Torah or the New Testament. One does not need to think. One needs just to follow instructions.

The other extreme response is hedonism. No rules whatsoever. No boundaries. Just go with the flow.

The common denominator in both cases is that there is no need to think.

Yes, it is becoming more and more difficult to think clearly. Finding common sense is becoming more and more rare. And yet people who can clear their minds to think with common sense are not appreciated. They are too simple minded, I am told.

Simple is powerful.

Maybe the answer is not in being simple but in simplifying the problem.

The more complex the problem, the harder we should work on simplifying it in order to understand it, and the more willing we should be to take the time and make the effort to find common sense by listening to others who do not necessarily agree with us from whom we can learn.

Seeking common sense is not so common in the complex world we live in, but, it is the right answer to deal with the complexities we are faced with.

Look for What You Do Not See[1]

I AM BECOMING AWARE of a certain phenomenon I had not paid attention to until now: There is complementarity in everything. The yin-yang combination is everywhere.

Practitioners of ayurvedic medicine recommend a diet of food that is complementary to ones style. Thus, a person comparable to the (E) style in ayurveda should eat food that (P)s prefer in order to balance his style, and (P)s should eat the foods that (A)s prefer.

Look at marriage: It is a complementary system, and it does not stop with the husband and wife; it also includes the children. If, for instance, the husband is a big (E) and the wife is a big (A), the first-born will develop the (I) style, and the second-born a (P) style.

Often, over a casual dinner with a couple I've recently met and have been observing, I have predicted the behavior of their children. Invariably, the couple has confirmed my description of their children's behavior; they always wonder how I knew.

Complementarity is not just among people or food.

Forty-four years ago, in writing my doctoral dissertation, I noted that a successful democratic organizational system needs strong, opinionated (i.e., dictatorial) leadership, while a dictatorial (i.e., totalitarian) system thrives under democratic-style, open-minded, "benevolent" leadership. A democratic system with a democratic style of leadership can produce extremes of anarchy or paralysis. Dictatorial leadership within a totalitarian system produces destructive dictators, such as Hitler and Stalin.

I believe there should be complementarity of style and system, of process and structure, of form and function. If the function is flexible, the form

1. Adizes Insights, January 2012.

has to be inflexible. If the form is ambiguous, the function has to be deterministic.

If you want to be understood quickly, speak slowly; and if you speak fast, you will be understood slowly.

Complementarity is everywhere. Look at the weather. The climate above the equator complements the climate below: When it is winter in New York, it is summer in Rio. When it is daylight in the western part of the globe, it is night in the eastern part.

If that is all true, does it mean that there is no good without the bad? No God without the devil? No love without hate?

If we excel at one task, must we necessarily be deficient at something else?

Does every saint have (hopefully under control) a devil in hiding somewhere in their personality?

Like the moon, the lit side has its counterpart dark side. The lighter one side is, the darker its complementary side will be.

WHO GETS THE MOST
GIVES THE LEAST¹

I'VE MADE THE FOLLOWING OBSERVATION, which has been substantiated over the years by events I've witnessed: The child who is given the most preference of all the kids is the one who takes the least care of his or her parents.

A friend of mine was telling me about the problem he has with one of his brothers. The middle brother was always very sick when he was young. Their mother worried endlessly about him surviving. She gave all her attention to this child at the expense of the other two. This middle brother grew up to be a very successful businessman and, of the three, he is the wealthiest, but when the time comes to support the parents, he always has an excuse for why he cannot do much.

This is an example, but not a lone one; in my experience it repeats itself many times.

Children learn: Do they only take, or do they have to give, too?

If children are raised by a maid who cleans their room, folds their laundry, and cooks all their meals, but cannot afford the maid as an adult, that child is not capable of coping well with the world. It appears as if this grown-up child needs a "babysitter" all his or her life. They are taught to expect preferential treatment even when it is not available or affordable.

Thus it is important that children be given assignments around the house, that they must contribute, whatever their capability, depending on their age. They must learn to give and not only to take.

And the giving should not stop at the boundaries of the family.

In the Jewish tradition, there is a donation box on the table where kids

1. Adizes Insights, January 2012.

put some money every Friday evening, as a contribution to build the Jewish country of Israel.

Kids need to learn to give from an early age if they are going to become productive members of society.

The Sahaj Marg mission's living Master says that love is like a muscle: You need to exercise it. The more you love the more you are able to love.

Generosity is one form of expressing love that needs to be developed; it needs to be exercised. It does not automatically happen when a person becomes wealthy enough to believe that he can afford to be generous.

I have noticed that generosity and wealth are not necessarily correlated. Some very wealthy people are stingy and some relatively poor people are generous.

People generally do what they learn at home from an early age.

To love and to give, to be generous with your belongings and with your emotions, is not an inherited trait but a learned habit. And the earlier you learn, the sooner you realize what it means to be human.

Why Not to Expect or Want[1]

I BELONG TO A SPIRITUAL MISSION, the Sahaj Marg. We meditate. We have a Master who teaches mostly by giving a personal example. I just spent a week in India and was honored to stay at his home and have personal sittings with him. I write this essay in his honor.

The meditation starts with a prayer, which has a certain part I want to focus on in this essay. It says, "for all we are is slaves to expectations."

The prayer directs us to free ourselves of expectations. Why? Because expectations and wishes enslave. They put our mind into the future, not in the present. The future is, by definition, not now. It moves. All the time. So do our wishes. We have new ones. So we are never fulfilled, never happy. There is always something else we wish for.

Here is a true story that makes the point: There is a bar in Amsterdam that has a big banner on its wall that says "Free Drinks Tomorrow."

If you truly believe it, you will come to the bar every day and never be satisfied: The free drinks are always not today, they are tomorrow."

By focusing on the future we miss the present. And we should focus on the present because that is what is real. The past is no more. And the future is not yet.

This focus on the present has its support in the Jewish religion, too. That is how I interpret the name of God in Hebrew: *Ye hoveh*. *Ye* refers to "in the future" and *hoveh* means "present, now." Thus the name of God, which observant Jews are prohibited to pronounce, means to me: "make your future now, be in the now."

If we do not have wishes, no expectations, we will notice and realize that

---

1. Adizes Insights, March 2013.

what we have in the present is all we need. The book of the Jewish sages says the same: *Mi hu ha meushar. Ha sameah be helko.* Who is happy? The one who is satisfied with what he or she has.

So, no more wishful thinking. Be happy. Take it as it comes.

Okay, but how about "wanting?"

When you want something, you are actually saying that you are not happy with what you have and you want something else.

Back to making yourself unhappy, by simply wanting. But, if you stop wanting, does it not make you "a vegetable?" You do not plan. You do not aim. Thus, you probably do not move and improve your life. You accept the same condition you started with.

Not to want is "sacrilegious," especially for a consultant, which is my profession. We always start by asking a client, "What do you want? What do you expect?" How otherwise?

The Master directed me to look at the natural way, which is the literal translation of the words "Sahaj Marg." When you go to the bathroom, do you want to go to the bathroom or do you need to go to the bathroom? You naturally go to the bathroom. How about breathing? You do not even think about it. You just breathe.

Imagine living your life that way. You do what needs to be done. Not because you wish something or want something. You do it because that is what needs to be done. You respond to a need and get your ego out of the way. You become a vehicle to deliver what needs to be delivered and you stop being self-driven. You serve instead.

Look at real artists. Gifted artists. They do not want to dance; they dance. Paint. Play music. Because they need to do it. They would die inside, their soul would die, otherwise. It would dry out like a flower with no water.

If you are a jazz musician and improvise you do not think. You do not plan the improvisation. You just play what you are inspired to play. You are a vehicle for the sounds to be played. If you a sculptor, you might plan what the stone is eventually going to be, but you'd better relax your wishes and wants and expectations. The stone provides you with a reality you need to respond to and eventually create what needs to be created. You need to take your ego out of the way or you will create a lousy piece of commercial art.

That brings me to the word "expectation." Expectation is more than wanting or wishing. It has a component of control in it. When you expect something it means that you give it probability that it should happen, which means that you expect it to be controllable. When an expectation does not get realized, we are very frustrated because it points to our weaknesses, to our helplessness.

By expecting nothing, we surrender.

Surrendering does not mean we are inactive, that we become vegetables.

We do our best. We do what needs to be done with all the passion and love and efforts we possess. And then we let it be. We expect nothing. We wish nothing. We want nothing. We let providence, nature, God, probabilities (if you are a statistician)...whatever you believe in, take its course. We have done our thing. No more. No less. We are complete. And thus we are happy.

I am practicing this philosophy of life. Working on it. It is not easy. Especially because I am Jewish and we Jews are in our heads all the time, thinking, planning, wanting, expecting. Very intense.

I am working hard through meditation to cut out wishful thinking, wanting, and expecting. I do not expect my books to be best sellers. I do not even write them in a way that I want them to be best sellers. If they are, good. And if not, fine too. I did what I could do. I did my best. That is all that is controllable by me. The rest is up to forces I have no control over.

I found out something fascinating by following this prayer. When you expect nothing and want nothing, whatever new happens is a surprise. Even bad surprises have a silver lining to them. Life becomes very interesting. You become a child again. There is something new to learn all the time. Life becomes richer. And, like a child, you smile more. You are happier. Less frustrated. Less demanding of others.

Nikos Kazantsakis, the author of *Zorba the Greek*, has this epigraph on his tomb in Crete: "No more fear, no more hope. Finally free." But, you do not need to die to be free. You can be free while still alive. Just stop wishing and wanting and expecting. You will be happy, like the Buddha was, with what is. Totally conscious of the now. No energy spent on the future, fighting the present to get to that elusive future. All your energy will be available now. All energy focused on now. Not on the past and not on the future. Now.

With no wishes and no expectations we get more powerful and closer to God. How? God is the most powerful being, I suggest to you, because God has no wishes and no expectations. God gave up expecting and wanting early in the Old Testament. With the flood, God realized He cannot make us righteous. He actually surrendered. He shows us the way, but He does not take control of our lives, even a bit. Thus, we cannot blame Him for the death of a loved one, or for the Holocaust, or for whatever happens to us. He did not do anything. He is there just watching. He just gave us the rules and watches to see whether we are following them or not. Observing with no judgment. With no anger. He controls nothing. The world goes its way. The world He (or She) created runs its course, governed by rules God has created, and that is the end of it.

If He surrenders, who are we not to?

About the Adizes Institute

For the past forty years, the Adizes Institute has been committed to equipping visionary leaders, management teams, and agents of change to become champions of their industries and markets. These leaders have successfully established a collaborative organizational culture by using Adizes' pragmatic tools and concepts to achieve peak performance.

Adizes specializes in guiding leaders of organizations (CEOs, top management teams, boards, owners) to quickly and effectively resolve such issues as:

- Difficulties in executing good decisions.
- Making the transition from entrepreneurship to professional management.
- Difficulties in aligning the structure of the organization to achieve its strategic intent.
- "Bureaucratizing"—the organization is getting out of touch with its markets and beginning to lose entrepreneurial vitality.
- Conflicts among founders, owners, board members, partners, and family members.
- Internal management team conflicts and "politics" severe enough to inhibit the success of the business.
- Growing pains.
- Culture clashes between companies undergoing mergers or acquisitions.

Adizes also offers comprehensive training and certification for change leaders who wish to incorporate into their practice the Adizes Methodologies for managing change.

Adizes is the primary sponsor of the Adizes Graduate School, a non-profit teaching organization that offers Master's and Ph.D. programs for the Study of Leadership and Change.

For more information about these and other programs, please visit www.adizes.com.

Adizes
INSTITUTE WORLDWIDE